Celebrating Festivals with Children

# Celebrating Festivals with Children

Freya Jaffke

Floris Books

Sections on Halloween and Thanksgiving by Stephen Spitalny
Illustrations by Christiane Lesch & Karl Drabowski
Photographs by Freya Jaffke, Thomas Klink & Charlotte Fischer

Translated by Matthew Barton

First published in German by Verlag Freies Geistesleben, Stuttgart in two
volumes under the titles: *Feste in Kindergarten und Elternhaus: Teil 1:
Jahreszeitentische, Advent, Weihnachten, Fasching* (2007)
and *Teil 2: Ostern, Pfingsten, Johanni, Michaeli, Lanternenfest* (1994)
First published in English by Floris Books, Edinburgh in 2011
Third printing 2022

British Library CIP Data available
ISBN 978-086315-832-2

# Contents

Publisher's Note

The perspective and the choice of festivals in this book reflects the time and place in which it was written: late twentieth-century Germany. The author encourages readers to adapt the traditions discussed here to new places, and to take on new and varied festival traditions.

# Foreword

Informed by the nature of different cultures and national characteristics, festivals are celebrated throughout the world in many diverse ways. Originally established in contexts of ritual worship, where they were considered to be profoundly significant, they have increasingly become mere tradition and routine. Today we feel a need to understand such traditions again and to enshrine them in more conscious celebration. It is therefore with much gratitude that we can consult publications that offer new insights into seasonal festivals and ways of celebrating them. You will find a useful selection in the 'Bibliography and Further Reading' section (p. 145).

The aim of this book is to describe festival celebrations in relation to child development in the first seven years. Young children are wide open, with all their senses, to what happens around them in the world, absorbing things deeply and grasping meaning initially through imitative action. It is up to adults, therefore, to visibly embody, in gestures which reveal their stance and outlook, what they can discover in order to understand the content of a festival. It is our particular concern to convey a love for the details which become so infinitely important when we live and work with children.

Our intention when we celebrate festivals is that they remain simple and appropriate, that children can share in preparing them, and that they do not overtax children by going on too long. However ceremonial festivals may be, it is good for them to have a healthy rhythmic dynamic, with lighter and more informal moments too.

In order to help deepen our relationship with festivals and re-enliven them continually as we celebrate them with children, this book offers a short prologue for adult reflection before each seasonal celebration. Since the nature table is so important when celebrating festivals, the first chapter is devoted in detail to this theme.

If we take a look at the whole rhythm of the year, the midwinter festival (Christmas) is balanced by a midsummer festival (St John's), and the spring festival (Easter) by an autumn one (Michaelmas). The inner connection of these festivals to each other and to the year's cycle can be studied in more depth in anthroposophy. This also offers us insights into child development, which can guide us in celebrating festivals with children of different ages.

Apart from festivals linked to the seasons, the latter part of this book looks at two events of major importance that are intimately connected with our personal biography, though not with the year's cycle. These are the festival of our birth, which we repeatedly celebrate throughout our lives, and the event of death that is here called our 'heavenly birthday'. Questions and uncertainties regarding the latter moved us to say a little about it.

This book aims to stimulate ideas and lively discussion about the many different ways in which festivals might be celebrated in kindergarten or at home, rather than to give fixed guidelines. I am deeply indebted to my colleagues who worked with me on this book: Johanna-Veronika Picht, Erika Kraft, Astrid Ahrens and Dr Helmut von Kügelgen.

*Freya Jaffke*

# The Seasonal Nature Table

## *Creating a seasonal nature table*

If we wish to follow the changing seasons at the same time as celebrating Christian festivals, the seasonal nature table is particularly important. Nature's gifts and the messages of the festivals come together here in a subtle and resonant way. On the one hand, we are giving our loving attention to all that flourishes and fades outdoors, and on the other we are seeking to understand more profoundly what happened 2,000 years ago at the time of Christ, and can still have living meaning. Trying to understand festivals more deeply in this way can enable us to draw on the world's mysteries and render them visible for children. Young children experience the world around them through a wealth of recurring sense impressions: they experience things directly, all the more so when they are not explained intellectually or 'taught' to them. As children grow older, their awakening souls will slowly find their way into ever-new meanings and connections.

At home and in kindergarten, a seasonal nature table – when properly created and experienced – can become a living source that enriches and refreshes us daily, stimulating our creative imagination for festive times.

Through preparation, then the culmination of a celebration itself, followed by the gentle reverberation as it fades, we can gain a sense of vibrant, rhythmical life.

Let us now look in detail at how a seasonal nature table (it can also be a little cupboard or chest of drawers) can be arranged.

## The coloured background

Firstly place a coloured cloth or blanket on the table to accentuate the seasonal mood. Considering the interplay of light and dark through the seasons can help us choose colours. Colours arise in the encounter between light and darkness, as we can see by studying Goethe's *Theory of Colours* or observing sunrises and sunsets. The first lightening of darkness produces violet blue, passing over more and more into blue as the light increases – which gradually grows more delicate. On the other hand, the first darkening of light gives rise to yellow and, as it deepens, to orange and red. Where lightened darkness (blue) encounters darkened light (yellow) we find green. Where deeply darkened light (red) meets the slightly brightened darkness (violet blue), purple is created.

During winter we have the most darkness, and at Christmas already its first lightening in blue. Fresh green corresponds to spring and Easter; summer and St John's to yellow; the autumn and Michaelmas to a radiant, warm red. If you feel like changing the undercloth more often, you can choose corresponding intermediary colours. Another way of doing this is to enrich the colour scheme by using delicate silk cloths in graduated or complementary colour tones.

## Nature's gifts

Upon this coloured background assemble gifts of nature from the plant and mineral kingdoms that can be found through the cycle of the year. It isn't a matter of collecting as much as possible but rather of finding things that seem to represent a particular season especially well.

In the early spring, for instance, this could be a couple of bare branches whose buds are slowly turning green; then delicate spring flowers and catkins, followed by daffodils, tulips and forget-me-nots. At Ascension and Whitsun we have meadow flowers and many white blossoms. At St John's come roses, and then the bright array of summer flowers. In autumn there are golden-yellow ears of corn, shining, colourful leaves and fruits, and glorious sunflowers. In late autumn we can find knotty roots, a little dry moss and lichens. At Christmas the seasonal table can host the crib and stable and later on, as winter gradually fades away, it can have a few beautiful stones, maybe even crystals, on a delicate blue background with a white veil.

But the small things that children bring so gleefully in from outside can find a worthy place here too. It might be a daisy, a snail shell or a pebble, beautifully coloured leaves, autumn fruits, a bird's nest and much more.

*Caring for the nature table*

The seasonal nature table will need a little daily care. There shouldn't be too much on it, so we can always take in at a glance what's there. Wilting plants should be removed or replaced; the undercloth will need to be shaken out from time to time. All this can be done with the children, as young children have a special perception for all these small labours of preparation and care, and naturally absorb them imitatively into their activities. Of course a seasonal table can also sometimes be tended without the children, but involving them in its care will enhance their interest and relationship with it. Often a child will stand before the table just looking and wondering. Once, when there were already several conkers, acorns and acorn cups on the table, a five-year-old boy brought in a horse chestnut in its green shell, with the stalk still attached. The shell had burst open a little, revealing the shining conker inside. By the end of playtime the warmth in the room had made the shell open wide. The boy took out the conker, gripped the stalk and, looking at the two halves of the shell said, 'Look, now it's turned into a butterfly.'

*Pictures on the nature table*

At festive times we like to place a relevant picture or art postcard on the table. I will discuss this in more detail in connection with each festival. In general all I would say here is that in kindergarten we choose pictures based on the children's understanding rather than adult perceptions, whereas at home it's fine to take the needs of older siblings into account.

## A deeper understanding of the nature table

Let's now consider how we as adults can come to a greater understanding both of natural occurrences through the seasons and also of their connection with Christian festivals. We can look for broader perspectives that guide us in creating a seasonal table. Anthropomorphism, for instance through humanised figures in the plant kingdom, is not recommended. Broader perspectives can come to expression in a conscious reticence or humility, guided initially by Rudolf Steiner's insights. Here we find diverse avenues for intensifying our study through the years. For instance, we can pursue the idea of the significance of the earth within its universal context, its relationship with surrounding regions of the cosmos. We can consider how the earth itself, as a living, ensouled organism, includes human beings in its great cycles of respiration, as these are revealed in the changing seasons.[1]

Besides studying lectures on the seasons and festivals, a fitting sense of the wonders of nature can also be engendered by accompanying the year through the words of Rudolf Steiner's *Calendar of the Soul*.[2] Repeatedly engaging with its 52 verses for each week of the year can increasingly help us to experience the connection between outward seasonal phenomena and our own soul. Likewise, poems, for example by Shakespeare, Wordsworth, Goethe, Novalis, Morgenstern or Robert Frost can give us a vivid sense of the changing moods of nature through the seasons.

## *The child's relationship to the nature table*

Young children still have an original and direct connection with nature. With joyful glee, for instance, they discover dew glinting in the sunshine or raindrops on a leaf, or they squat before a hole in the earth from which a worm is slowly emerging, or watch entranced as a snail creeps along slowly with its house on its back. They may follow the flight of a bee from blossom to blossom, or shiver with delight when a little ladybird comes winging its way to settle on their arm or hand. Rapt, they will spread out their arms and run after wind-blown leaves. Invariably children's attention is drawn by distinct events and movements in their immediate environment rather than by the beautiful mood of a sunset or the view over a deep valley. To learn to love and value nature's beauty in ever deeper ways, children need examples. They best learn to develop respect and care for nature through an adult's interest or enthusiasm. In imitation of the adult they can find wonder in their surroundings and learn to love and cherish them.

The urge to destroy in some children can also be overcome by this means. One child, who only a few weeks earlier had stepped wantonly on a spider, discovered a large spider's web glittering in the sun, and fluttering lightly in the wind, with its many tiny drops of dew. Excitedly he called his kindergarten teacher over to show them. We can guide a child's connection with nature further by bringing nature indoors and creating a seasonal table. If we do this out of our own profound experience of nature, this can help lay a foundation in children which enables them to find their own connection between the cycle of the seasons and the Christian festivals.

# Winter

# Advent and Christmas

## *Creating the mood ourselves*

The Christmas festival represents the fulfilment of a process that unfolds very quietly through many months. From the full light and warmth of high summer, the soul withdraws increasingly into itself as the light gradually diminishes. The moment of equilibrium between light and dark in autumn is like a threshold over which we pass; and at the darkest time of the year an inner light can be kindled. If we are really to celebrate Christmas, we need to make renewed efforts every year to internalise outward light and transform it, so that it shines out from within us. Then others will sense peace, love and warmth emanating from us like a blessing – the arrival of Christ in our soul. Advent means both approach and arrival (from the Latin *advenire)* and this means that we can try again each year, as far as we are able, to allow the great, divine being who committed himself to humanity on earth through the event of Golgotha, to approach and arrive in us.

We all know that we can only accomplish this through inner composure, at quiet moments when we manage to step aside from daily life. But equally we know how outward frantic preparations can make such composure particularly difficult in the run-up to Christmas. Yet the children whose surroundings we create, and for whom we organise festivals, will reward us with their daily happiness and loyalty, encouraging us to persevere.

Engaging with a beautiful verse is one way of making good use, as adults, of the odd quiet moment. Focusing on this verse each day for just a few minutes can imbue our day with its content and help us to find the right attitude towards our work as carers.

Perhaps, if we do so, a sudden realisation will dawn, or a little insight strike us, or maybe we will simply feel more enthusiastic. Young children can experience this subtle shift – not in words but through our gestures and behaviour. Small children have a sure, though unconscious, sense of the thoughts and feelings we surround them with.

Below are a few appropriate verses for this time of year. But I'd like to stress that these are just some among many, and everyone should seek out their own.

### Prayer at the ringing of evening bells[3]

To wonder at beauty,
guard the truth,
honour what's noble,
resolve to do good:
this leads human beings
in life to their goal,
in deeds to what's right,
in feelings to peace,
in thinking to light;
and teaches them trust
in the workings of God
in all that exists
in the universe,
in the innermost soul.

*Rudolf Steiner*

### Christmas[4]

In eye of soul is mirrored
the hope of cosmic light,
spirit-affirming wisdom
speaks in the human heart:
the Father's infinite love
sends to earth the Son

who pours upon our human path
unstinting light of heaven.

*Rudolf Steiner*

**Light is love[5]**

Light is love ... sun-weaving
love radiance of a world
of creative beings –

who through unheard aeons
hold us to their heart, and who
at last into the frame of a man

gave us their loftiest spirit
for three years. He came
to thus inherit

His Father's work – and now has grown
to be earth's inmost heavenly fire so that
it too one day can be a sun.

*Christian Morgenstern*

Another way to prepare ourselves for the Advent and Christmas period is to consciously consider a range of virtues. Practising these on a small scale can even involve children. It would be wrong to draw their attention to meditative practice as such, but we can give them a sense of good habits through our example, which they will imitate and internalise.

Advent is the time of expectancy. Waiting for things is often hard for us: we want to get things over and done with and see quick results. Waiting teaches us to manage time differently. Wishes and preconceptions hurry us forward into the future, but to realise them we need time, duration; we must wait and overcome our impatience. Children can experience this waiting in the form of the Advent calendar, where only one door is opened each day; or when baking biscuits and cakes that may not be eaten until Christmas.

Listening is another virtue. We can only sense and cope with stillness and silence if we can listen. Perhaps we can listen with children to the silence of a forest, getting them to be quiet for a moment without discussing it. They will gladly listen quietly to a fairy tale or story, especially in convivial, familiar surroundings.

Looking during Advent can be directed particularly to the heavens: for instance at sunset after a fine day, when strong, luminous colours shine out; or a little later in the evening, when the winter stars seem unusually bright and close to the earth.

Finally there is the capacity for wonder, which we adults may often have to learn anew. There is so much to wonder at and admire as we sort through our collection of Christmas cards, becoming aware of the gestures and mood with which the shepherds or kings adore the child. Some pictures of the divine birth seem to show Mary in conversation with the baby Jesus. And when we assemble the nativity scene for children at school or at home, we can suddenly realise with wonder that all the realms of nature and the cosmos are greeting the child's arrival: stones from the mineral kingdom, moss, hay and straw from the plant realm, sheep, ox and ass from the animal kingdom, and then all the diversity of the human figures. The angel represents the higher worlds.

Wonder is the first step on the path to knowledge, and also involves deep respect for certain things. And so, when we're looking at the nativity scene with children, we can wonder at it, and avoid removing the crib figures for use as toys.

Each of us may find and nurture other virtues. It's not a matter of practising them all but of finding a way to guide children through the Advent period.

Let's now turn to the question of how we can enable children to participate, in a way that is right for them, in this inner preparatory work of the adult. It must always happen in a down-to-earth and joyous way, and invite their imitation or participation. Below I'll highlight a few possibilities.

## Preparation with children

In late autumn when the garden has been tidied and cleared, spring bulbs have been planted, the beds have been covered with brushwood and protective straw has been pulled around the rose bushes, we go out into the dusk with our lanterns and once again light up the secret corners where hedgehogs, little mice or gnomes have made their nests, holes and winter hideaways (see 'The lantern festival', p. 127).

But now the 'arrival' is to be prepared. If something is approaching we must make space for it. Just as we adults can try to take a moment out of the busy day to create a space for reflection and calming thoughts in the soul, so in kindergarten in the two weeks preceding the first day of Advent (which is the start of the festive period) the children's environment, room and toys can be thoroughly cleaned, and some things can be reorganised.

Below I offer suggestions for such cleaning activities from our work in the kindergarten. Children often carry away enthusiasm to inspire similar work at home.

### The big clean

We start by cleaning the wooden toys. All the little bowls and spoons from the dolls' corner, the shovels from the shop corner, and the wooden animals and trains are brought to the kitchen area. Here an adult stands before the electric stove and holds a cotton cloth lightly dipped in fluid beeswax (add around three to five drops of pure turpentine to a tablespoon of fluid wax) over the hotplate. Taking a wooden toy in the other hand, the old wax layer melts with the dirt that has accumulated, and is cleaned off with the cloth, and then re-waxed. The wooden object is turned until it has been cleaned all over. Watch out! Only apply a very thin layer of wax, if necessary rubbing off any excess with a clean, wax-free cloth over the hotplate, so that the toys do not become sticky afterwards. Clean toys are then placed on a nearby table, where the children gather to polish them with cloths.

cleaned, re-waxed and polished, the toys are placed in a basket and no longer used until the first day of Advent.

If you want to make this process a little easier, or don't have an electric hotplate at school, you can also rub down the wooden items with a good beeswax balsam and then polish them. Here again, only very little is needed.

### The big wash

The big clean continues with the big wash. All large play cloths are gratefully fed into our washing machine in the basement, or given to willing parents to wash at home. All small play cloths, dolls' blankets and sheets, woollen cords and ribbons are sorted by colour. The big metal bathtub is brought in and placed in the classroom, cloakroom, corridor or washroom – wherever is convenient. Into the warm soapsuds go the light-coloured cloths first of all, to be rubbed on a washboard or by hand. Children gather round to help with rolled-up sleeves, wearing aprons and possibly rubber boots. The six-year-olds are already reliable helpers while the four- and five-year-olds are more easily distracted by their enjoyment of water, soapsuds and the scrubbing brush, or by watching the spirals and gurgles of dirty water running down the plughole in the basin. If there aren't enough clothes racks for hanging up all the washing, we string some washing lines across the washroom and cloakroom, which gives washing days their own special atmosphere. The next day an adult will set up an ironing corner somewhere suitable. The small piles of beautifully sorted, ironed and folded cloths will be laid to one side and likewise await the first day of Advent.

### Cleaning the furniture

The furniture too is thoroughly cleaned. All chairs, stools, benches, tables, play stands and shelves are rubbed down with small amounts of beeswax balsam and polished. If this is done in an ordered and sequential way, it will offer all sorts of opportunities for the children to either join in and help, or for wonderful games. Furniture pushed together in unusual ways –

either after cleaning or awaiting it – can stimulate play: trains, cafés, ships, wagons etc.

Finally, the cupboards and drawers are cleaned. One drawer after another is cleared out, cleaned and re-stocked. Some of the most interesting areas for children are the tool cupboards and sewing drawers. Three- and four-year-olds love playing with the button boxes, while the older ones may be keener on sorting needles on a pin cushion by their coloured heads, or winding up thread reels more tightly.[6]

## Making an Advent wreath

The last day before Advent has arrived. A few table lanterns on the large, covered table and a lamp in the kitchen are all the light we need for our work today. Outside it's still dark. An adult is busy binding the Advent wreath, and the wonderful smell of fresh branches fills the air. A few children sit there too and pass small branches. Others – especially the older ones – cut off small sprays from the remaining branches and skilfully make their own little wreaths with them.

Ideally, we prefer to use fir branches for the Advent wreath. The very form of the tree emanates a strong, upright quality. In their shape fir branches embody both a striving upwards to the heavens and also a protective, downwards and earth-directed gesture. Small animals find safety there. We can rediscover these gestures in every single branch. The image of the fir tree can guide us into the Christmas mood – of seeking within ourselves for the connection between heaven and earth.

Our final task on this day is to fill the empty shelves with the newly cleaned things; then everything is ready for the approaching festive period. Any other special Advent preparations can be done without the children present; at Advent a time of secrecy and mysteries begins.

## Decorating the room for Advent

It's good to choose carefully from the huge range of possible room decorations for Advent. Advent is a time of preparation but not yet fulfilment. Too much decoration can distract us from essential things. Below are some suggestions that have worked well in practice, but they should not limit your own choices. Everything should not appear at once. The most important place in the room will always no doubt be the seasonal nature table with the crib scene.

### The nativity scene on the nature table

All sorts of things are possible when arranging the Advent nature table and nativity scene. It's good to keep reviewing our decisions in this regard and share experiences with colleagues, and also to feel inwardly connected with whatever we decide to do, so that children experience it as authentic.

The wall behind the nature table is often decorated with a blue cloth from the first of Advent. We usually hang a picture of Raphael's *Sistine Madonna* there, and she now has a blue background. On the table itself, the Christmas story with crib figures can now gradually unfold. The landscape for this can be created with cloths and moss. To make a moss landscape, an edged board is a good idea, lined with silver foil. Under the moss a thin layer of earth is laid so that the moss stays fresh for longer, and so that tiny trees or a pot plant can be planted there. The moss retains its vigour and its aromatic forest smell if finely sprayed with water at least once a day. Sometimes delicate little leaves or grass stalks start growing out of it. It's nice if the landscape is a little bit hilly. Here and there, crystals can glitter amidst the moss.

Space should be left somewhere for the stable, which can be made of pieces of bark and a straw roof, or branches or just bark. The floor can be strewn with straw, with a small corn sheaf in one corner. A gnome may be poking his face out of the green moss in the background, representing the burgeoning elemental world whose beings participate in the forthcoming event of Christ's birth.

A winding path leads to this stable, made for instance of dried pine needles or small stones. In this landscape, gradually building up through the Advent period, the Christmas events can now slowly unfold. On the first of Advent maybe only a single candle burns, to one side where the first shepherd can be seen with one sheep. Each day another sheep can be added, and gradually the other shepherds join the first. We give them the names they have in the Oberufer Christmas plays:[7] Huckle, Muckle, Gallus and Crispus. Choose any suitable names. Once the first three have gathered, for one day the angel appears on the hill to bring them the Christmas message. The next day the shepherds set off on their journey, timed to arrive at the stable on the last day of the kindergarten term. (They will leave again when the children are not present.) The sheep left behind are cared for by the fourth shepherd.

In the meantime, Mary and Joseph are journeying too, with the ox and ass, from the other direction. (The ox and ass can of course also be added later once Mary and Joseph have arrived at the stable.)

On the last day of term before the Christmas holidays, everyone has arrived at the stable. This is also the day when we celebrate a festival with the parents (see 'Christmas in kindergarten', p. 50). And so, to complete the picture, the baby Jesus may now also be placed in the manger.

### Alternatives for the nativity scene

In some kindergartens, Mary and Joseph start their journey on the first day of Advent, and the shepherds only come later. Or the annunciation to Mary marks the beginning; or there may be a path formed of golden stars on which Mary progresses from one star to the next each day. Each star that she passes appears the following day pinned to the blue cloth on the wall.

At home children and parents may wish to build the nativity scene together. On a walk you can collect moss and other small treasures, and on the day before Advent form these into a landscape. Perhaps a pretty stone, a candle and the first figures appear overnight so that something mysterious happens alongside your shared preparations. This, as well as the inner certainty of the adults, and the example perhaps of older siblings, can invoke real wonder in young children; and it then becomes self-evident that we do not take crib figures off the table and play with them. Sometimes the moss landscape is still fairly bare on the first day of Advent, and with every new day there is something new to be discovered – for instance a stone, a plant, a fir cone or a new figure.

Some families have a tradition whereby a further realm of nature is added each Sunday in Advent: on the first day of Advent stones and crystals, on the second plants or flowers, on the third the animals, and on the fourth the human figures.

Some may question whether it is right that the annunciation to the shepherds is portrayed in Advent, since it is a Christmas Eve event; or that the child is placed in the crib several days before Christmas, on the last day of term; or that the annunciation to Mary is in winter. No doubt we should not do these things arbitrarily, and we should keep considering such questions. But being too fixed or dogmatic about it isn't good either. On the last day of term when the picture is complete, with shepherds and child, one can sense the children's deep satisfaction. For the older children this fulfilment is absolutely understandable, since the shared experience of Advent culminates and concludes when school ends. They have no trouble with the fact that at home, for instance, the child will only appear in the crib on Christmas Eve. The younger children, for their part, just observe it all unquestioningly and joyfully.

### A source for the future

Irrespective of different ways of creating the Advent table, this humble little scene unfolds before the children a tableau which, without thinking about it intellectually, they can connect with through a range of sense impressions.

Later, when they try to plumb the mysteries of the world in their thoughts, they may become aware how this picture gathers together the whole of Creation – stone, plant, animal, human being and angels – to welcome into its midst the new, renewing light of the world. Young children should be allowed to live and grow with such pictures, from day to day and year to year. Later, at school, the wonderful images from the Oberufer plays are added,[8] from whose deep fount children and adolescents can draw throughout their lives. Indeed, they can become a source of strength and perhaps at special moments light up in the soul and shine out beyond all the stresses of daily life.

## Advent calendars

To experience the progression through the Advent period with still greater awareness, and make the approach of the Christmas festival more visible, a wide range of Advent calendars have been created. I will mention only a few of the many possibilities. I'm sure no one will think of using all of these at once in their children's bedroom or in kindergarten.

Even in a big family not every child needs to have their own Advent calendar but can instead wait their turn in the most natural way and thus practise patience. Fathers and mothers can participate in this daily ritual in the case of only children.

### An Advent calendar with doors[9]

An Advent calendar that you hang up in a window or put on the windowsill is especially lovely. With each door they open, children see how the light of the sky or a candle shines in more strongly and illuminates everything. Homemade calendars are no doubt the best, allowing us to choose and order each motif into a larger context of meaning.

Similarly, transparencies invoke this light phenomenon and are often placed in a window or in front of a candle during Advent and Christmas. Just as the light shines in and shines through, and lends all physical things a special glow, so love can embrace and permeate our lives. Transparencies remind us of this particularly at this time.

### An Advent clock

This clock is not one with hands that point to symbols, but is made of two interpenetrating cardboard discs. It was conceived and developed by Anke Usche-Clausen.

By turning the discs round a little more each day, the angle continually increases to reveal ever more of the large, unified nativity scene which finally appears complete.

Unlike the many small windows of the Advent calendar, which as far as possible should form a meaningful whole together, here a new detail of a single, large picture becomes visible with every passing day.

*A walnut chain*

A walnut chain is a quite different kind of Advent calendar. It consists of empty walnut shells painted gold, their two halves are stuck to either side of a long red ribbon, which connects the separate nuts and seals their shells shut; each holds a little secret inside. It's important to always use whole shells (two halves together) and not just stick half nutshells onto the ribbon. The point is to open the nut and find its hidden 'kernel'.

In kindergarten, of course, the number of nuts on the ribbon is determined by the number of children in the group and not by the days of Advent. Each child has a turn at cutting off a nut; we always start with the youngest rather than the best behaved. The kindergarten teacher will find some way to ensure that all children have received a nut before Christmas comes.

At the point in the day assigned for this, perhaps at midday before the final song, when all the children have gathered in front

nativity scene, the teacher cuts a nut off the ribbon (in some groups the children themselves may do this). The teacher sits close to the children and carefully opens the nut, then places it in the hand of the child whose turn it is. The child then slowly walks past all the others to let them see what is inside the nut. The nut is sealed again with a little beeswax, and the child takes it home.

The nuts can contain something different each day in a repeating sequence, for instance: a little bell, a small gnome with a tiny crystal, a doll's bed covered in felt, a little sailing ship (press a small ball of beeswax into the shell, and push in a sail made of half a matchstick and some fabric), three small candles, a little lamb made of teased sheep's wool, a little shepherd or another figure, or a bag containing tiny crystals.

At home the nut chain could contain everything needed for a small nativity scene, so that children may slowly assemble their own little scene in their room.

In kindergarten it would also be possible for the same thing to be in the nut every day, which might be beneficial if a group is new and has not yet grown together properly.

*Angel letters*

'Angel letters' can also be a kind of Advent calendar. These are white envelopes decorated with a golden star, containing a beautiful picture or art postcard on a Christmas theme. They are hung up on a blue cloth on the wall by a golden thread that runs under the envelope's flap. A child opens one each day, and the picture, with the child's name on the back, is pinned to the cloth. As the days progress, there are more and more pictures and fewer and fewer letters left. On the last day of term all the cards have been taken down, and each one has been fixed to gold cardboard and wrapped up as a present for the children to take home with them.

## Moss gardens

At the beginning of Advent we create a little moss garden with every child. A pottery bowl (around 16–20 cm, 6–8 in wide) is filled with earth and covered with a layer of moss. The bowls are standing on the windowsill, with names attached, by December 5 at the latest. On December 6, St Nicholas brings each child a little branch with a golden star or small crystal attached. The sight of the gold star amidst the green is an image of the heavenly forces uniting with the earth in a special way at Advent. Twigs are brought by St Nicholas in a little basket, which we call the 'basket of secrets'. This basket has the magic property of refilling itself: it stands in the allotted place, covered with a cloth, and new 'treasures' for the moss garden are brought each day by St Nicholas's 'helpers'. Such treasures might be a larch cone, a white feather, a sprig from a juniper tree that looks like a tiny tree, a shell, an acorn cup, a maple seed, an ear of corn and, shortly before Christmas, a golden walnut shell intended as a manger for the baby.

At the end of the Advent period we push a few fir twigs into the moss in a semi-circle as a background for the scene.

On the penultimate day of term we wrap the little gardens in a large piece of tissue paper to enclose them in a festive way and at the same time protect them.

In some kindergartens, instead of wrapping up the gardens, a candle is pushed into the moss and lit at the end of the festival we celebrate with parents. The children then carry their moss gardens with burning candles to their parent or carer (see 'Christmas in kindergarten', p. 50).

Throughout Advent most children and parents feel strongly connected to these little moss gardens. Some children rearrange their garden each day after watering it, and add things they find themselves. During the Holy Nights at home, children will often continue to feel drawn to it. The moss garden represents, on a small scale, what children experience with the large nativity scene on the nature table: that the events of Christmas have significance for all of Creation.

We make little crib figures out of beeswax for these gardens.

*Beeswax figures*

In the last few days before the Christmas holidays, we put a bowl containing pure, yellow beeswax into the oven. For the recipe see this note.[10] At a moderate heat of around 50°C (120°F) the wax stays beautifully warm and supple, and we can keep taking what we need from the bowl.

The teacher sits at a table near the children and starts forming small Mary and Joseph figures around 5 cm (2 in) high – in the simplest possible way, without any details. A few children will quickly join in and start shaping their own figures if you let them simply imitate freely, without any 'requirements'. Three- and four-year-old children, who participate in their own way by energetically pressing the wax and moving it from one hand to another, will after a while happily receive figures made for them by the teacher or older children, and carry them to their garden. It is important that the younger children participate freely and happily in the others' activity, and do not lose their pleasure through inappropriate demands or comparisons.

It can take several days before all the children have Mary and Joseph figures in their gardens.

At the very end we place the baby Jesus – made of a small, oval piece of wax with a round head and no features at all – into the walnut shell upholstered with a small tuft of sheep's wool.

### Advent singing

Advent is often the only time of year when families sing together. Singing really connects people in a community and for this reason many kindergartens organise Advent singing sessions. To take proper account of children's needs, this should be done in not too large a group, for not too long, and above all not too often, so children don't lose too much of their precious playtime. For this reason, many kindergartens restrict it to one Advent preparation session. In our school it takes place soon after we start in the morning. Children from two classes, and parents who can come, join together. To begin with, though, the children gather round their teacher, who will be sitting by a lit candle, perhaps teasing wool or looking at a picture book in an adjoining room or in the hallway. The parents sit down quietly with them and settle into the easy, peaceful mood of waiting. At the agreed time, everyone goes together into one of the two classrooms and sits in a semi-circle in front of the nature table nativity scene (see p. 26).

Apart from well-known Advent and Christmas songs, we also sing pentatonic Advent songs. After about ten minutes we put out the candles on the Advent wreath and the moss gardens, the parents leave and the children's free-play period begins.

In some kindergartens, several groups meet for Advent singing, perhaps even standing in a hallway to sing as candles burn on an Advent wreath. Here, too, care is taken that the children stand together with their teacher. What adults experience as a convivial social gathering in a large group is something young children find, instead, in a smaller group of familiar people.

## *Advent spiral (or garden)*

Earlier we spoke of how, in preparation for Christmas, adults can try to create moments of peace for themselves (see p. 19). If we can manage to withdraw from outer, sensory experience into our inner world, we may occasionally be graced with clearer vision. Such a path inwards may often be difficult to find and can only be pursued out of our own free intent. And each year we have to try again. But continual effort of this kind, and progress by small steps, leads us to an authentic inner stance and composure which can come to expression in our actions and gestures.

Children can only embark on this process through outward activity. They still have quite a few preparatory steps to take before they will be capable of taking the path into the quiet of their inner soul.

Thus a lovely custom has developed in which, at the start of Advent, the children walk a big spiral on the ground, formed of fir branches or moss, at the centre of which stands a large candle where they light their own candle. The spiral has long been a Christian symbol of the path of the human soul to its own inmost centre.

### Preparing the spiral

A few practical aspects are important to consider when preparing this activity.

When laying the spiral with small fir branches or moss, we always take care to follow the path of the spiral itself rather than simply stepping over the branches already in place. Movements in space are a reality and leave invisible traces which the children may sense the following day.

The question arises as to which direction the spiral should be laid in – clockwise or anticlockwise. Personally I don't think this matters much, since reasons can be found for either.

Apart from a simple spiral it's also possible to lay a double one (see picture below). This came to our attention from an illustration of an Advent garden in a Camphill Community. Here we don't return by the same path as we entered but by one that runs parallel to it (follow the dotted line). Thus the adult accompanying the child can always stay behind the child. On the green spiral of fir branches, stars of gold cardboard (around 10 cm, 4 in wide) can be placed at regular intervals. These mark the places where the children place their candles. The children can take this star with them after putting their candle down.

The large candle in the middle – the Christmas light – from which the children light their own small candles, is surrounded by crystals. This seems a deeply significant image, giving children a tangible sense of going to a source from which their own light can grow as they themselves grow and develop. This spiral path of human soul development, dark at the start of the festival, is gradually illumined as one child after another places their light upon it.

*Candle apples*

The candle that children light in the Advent spiral is embedded in an apple. The apple, originally from the Tree of Knowledge, here becomes the bearer of light. This candle is a living light that can only spread light and warmth by giving up its own substance.

Red apples are polished to a fine shine and then a vertical hole, not too deep (around 2 cm, 3/4 in), is made in each with an apple corer. When inserting the candles they can be surrounded by very short fir tips or a rosette of gold foil. The apple candles are laid ready in a basket or on a tray on a small table by the entrance to the spiral.

*Safety precautions*

Once everything is ready, it's vital to have a bucket of water standing by, with damp cloths, at a hidden, easily accessible place. Before taking children into the Advent spiral we must make sure they are not wearing anything that's sticking out, like a scarf, which could catch fire. Tie up any loose or straggly hair with a hair clip.

*Walking the spiral*

When all the children are ready, and quiet, by the door, they are led into the room where they sit down on chairs around the spiral. The candle in the middle has been lit beforehand, and the tones of a lyre or children's harp are already playing.

Without telling a story – though this is certainly appropriate for older children – the kindergarten teacher first enters the spiral alone and lights their candle. Then they accompany one child after another into the spiral, perhaps placing a hand on the shoulder of the youngest children, and following behind the eldest with warm attentiveness. The children place their candle apples at the places marked by stars, then take the star with them out of the spiral and keep it in their hands.

The path from within outwards, it's worth saying, usually takes a long time to be illumined: light only slowly spreads from within. All the time the children are lighting their candles and walking the spiral, we sing a particular song – *Über Sterne, über Sonne* ('Over the stars, over the sun'). Of course, other, or several Advent songs can be sung. From time to time we pause with our singing as we have a sense that the spoken word, especially for older children, can have a calming and focusing effect, and we say the following star verse:

A star awakes, shines bright
In the depths of night,
Shimmers in the heavens above
Pours upon the world its love.
In the depths of night
A star awakes, shines bright.

Some children will quietly speak these words too, quite unselfconsciously. Once all the candles have been lit, including ones for absent or sick children, we wait a moment and then let the children walk back into the spiral a second time to pick up their candle and carry it out; or otherwise the adults collect the candles and bring them to each child. They hold the candle apple for a moment in both hands on their knees – not too close to the body (make sure they don't bend over the flames). We tell them that in the evening their mother and father can light the candle once more, and then the teacher goes from one child to another, gently extinguishing each light with a snuffer. Little lanterns placed here and there in the room ensure that it is not too dark, both when entering and leaving again.

It is equally lovely for the children to take away with them instead, as a final impression, the sight of the brightly lit spiral. Perhaps they can wait a moment or two and eat a piece of apple cake before they are led out again. In this case, the candle apples will be given to them afterwards, in another room. If they were still lit when they are given out, they can now be extinguished.

If parents are invited to this festival, it helps to explain its meaning and importance to them beforehand, and make sure they know what to expect, so that they can take part with the right kind of mood. A parent could accompany their child into the spiral instead of the teacher.

It's a good idea not to have too big a group of children in the room at any one time, so that the festival doesn't last more than half an hour. Sitting still any longer than that could prove too much for them. Different kindergarten groups can celebrate this festival at different times in the day, or one after another.

## St Nicholas

St Nicholas brings another true and resonant image to children on their journey through Advent. The St Nicholas festival is associated with a real historical individual who lived in the fourth century, not to be confused with the modern figure of Father Christmas, who has become associated with him (see also 'St Nicholas and Father Christmas' p. 44). Legends about St Nicholas describe how he emanated love and benevolence and was willing to sacrifice himself. Thus he became a figure who prepares and heralds the Christmas festival, at which the birth of Christ can be renewed in us each year.

### Costume and accessories

The figure of St Nicholas should be truthful, which includes his outward appearance. A white priest's garment with a golden belt indicates the purity of his being, and a blue star mantle his heavenly origins. On his head he wears a mitre, on his feet strong boots, for he must journey a long way upon the earth – although in some kindergartens he wears golden sandals. As an initiate he knows how to find the way into the inmost core of the human soul.

## The bishop's staff

St Nicholas holds a bishop's staff, at the upper end of which we find the involuted spiral, indicating once more the path, mentioned above, into the innermost human soul.

## The golden book

As an initiate, St Nicholas can see into cosmic and earthly circumstances. This is symbolised by the form of the golden – rather than ordinary – book he carries; for gold embodies a quality which we also, for instance, find in fairy tales as an indication of wisdom. In this book is written an objective account of everything that has happened. How we wish sometimes that something could be undone – but this cannot be. All we can do is try to compensate with good deeds for what has already happened.

St Nicholas is a herald of the baby Jesus, not a moralising figure or an imparter of requirements for children's upbringing. He perceives but does not judge, though he may express pleasure too. Since young pre-school children still live wholly in the present moment, it is best to read out events inscribed in the golden book that have happened in the last few days. After the age of seven, children can start reflecting on their actions and perhaps undertake to change or improve something. At that point St Nicholas, who always stands up for truth and addresses the good in us, can offer them help, but by appealing to their good will rather than by moralising.

### St Nicholas's gifts

The path we try to pursue towards Christmas is a path of will that can be taken both inwardly and outwardly. St Nicholas brings us the provisions for this journey, and so it is a good custom if he puts these provisions in the children's shoes – or in some traditions their stockings. There is meaning in the three gifts he brings: an apple as representative of all fruits and as memory of the Tree of Knowledge; nuts (preferably indigenous ones) which require some strength to get at the inner kernel – as children try to do with great enjoyment. Often, as adults, we may face a difficult problem and say, 'That's a hard nut to crack.' The third gift from St Nicholas is gingerbread or a baked cake, full of warming, enlivening ingredients. Other gifts, such as coloured pencils or toys, falsify the picture and turn St Nicholas into Father Christmas.

In our kindergarten St Nicholas brings his gifts in a large sack containing a small bag for each child. How he procures these little bags is described below.

## St Nicholas's bags

With parents' help we sew small red or blue bags (about 22 x 24 cm, 8 $^1/_2$ x 9 $^1/_2$ in). Red suggests the activity associated with the bags' contents, whereas blue indicates the aspect of a heavenly gift.

A few days before the first day of Advent, the children find a little package wrapped in gold paper in a secret corner of the kindergarten room. It contains as many pieces of cut-out fabric as there are new children in the group. A letter in gold writing asks the children's parents to sew a little bag out of the fabric, and embroider their child's name on it. Children may also bring little bags with them from home. They are wrapped up together and placed in front of the window, where St Nicholas's helpers can collect them. The children would love to catch a glimpse of the helpers, but they always come while we're out on a walk...

The person who is to represent St Nicholas will be told of all these preparatory thoughts and activities, so that he can fully identify with his task and play his part authentically.

### St Nicholas Day

The children look forward to St Nicholas's arrival with great expectancy and excitement. On the morning of December 6 we prepare a worthy chair for him to sit on, and place candles nearby. We push the furniture a little to one side so that we have plenty of space to arrange our chairs in a double semi-circle. The curtains are drawn, the candles burn and we sing. Suddenly someone is knocking at our door, and St Nicholas enters with great dignity. As he walks in a colleague brings in the big sack and puts it down.

Standing not too close to the children, St Nicholas tells of his star journey through the heavens, his meeting with Mother Mary and his descent to earth. After this he hands the teacher the basket of secrets (described on p. 33 in connection with the little moss gardens). Then he sits down and calmly opens the golden book. Slowly he reads out the name of each child and mentions recent events (to avoid this taking too long, groups of two or three children are mentioned together). The children often respond to this with an affirmative nod, a glance at the teacher and a few happily whispered words about what he has described. St Nicholas lovingly acknowledges any spontaneous comments from the children without many words. By singing a song that St Nicholas asks them to sing, they can now breathe out again fully after this hearkening 'in-breath'. Then the big sack is opened and the gifts are distributed. The kindergarten teacher helps St Nicholas to do this by taking the little bags out and handing them to him. The children come up, called by St Nicholas one by one, and he places the little bag into their two hands. If the child does not thank him, the teacher does instead, quite naturally, without this being any kind of prompt to the child. Hesitant children are guided by the teacher or an older child, or the little bag is brought to them.

Once all the children have received their bag, and another song has been sung, St Nicholas says farewell and continues on his journey, leaving behind him a bright glow in the children's souls.

In some places St Nicholas is accompanied by his servant Ruprecht, a dark and bent figure. He does not speak but only occasionally hums or mutters to himself. He is regarded as a necessary polarity to the dignified form of St Nicholas, ensuring with the odd humorous gesture that the occasion does not become too earnest. However, this duality can be dispensed with for pre-school children. At this age they can still give their undivided attention to the light-filled, upright figure of

# 44 CELEBRATING FESTIVALS WITH CHILDREN

St Nicholas, absorbing it through all their senses without being diverted or distracted.

Children are frequently confronted in their lives with the powers of darkness, of evil, without us being able to do anything about it. What we can do, though, is to provide protected spaces where the forces of good and truth can imbue them strongly enough to sustain them later in life.

Comparisons with wicked or dark figures in fairy tales, for example, are not relevant here, for they do not appear in physical form but are created in children's souls as they listen to stories, which subsequently always redeem, balance or overcome them.

There might be reasons not to have St Nicholas actually appear in person. In this case he may have arrived during the night, leaving a sack with a letter; or perhaps he came while we were out on a walk, and filled each child's stocking.

**The St Nicholas breakfast**

Today a few little baskets holding nutcrackers are standing on the tables. After the children have taken the gingerbread or the apple or both from their little bags, and also put a few hazelnuts and walnuts on their breakfast plates, a cheerful nut-cracking session begins, giving at least as much enjoyment as eating the nuts themselves. Five- and six-year-olds enthusiastically help the kindergarten teacher to crack nuts for the younger ones – who try to crack nuts too, but don't yet have sufficient strength or skill.

*St Nicholas and Father Christmas*

Finally I'd like to stress that it's important to maintain a clear distinction between St Nicholas and Father Christmas. 'Father Christmases' in red cloaks with friendly red cheeks, who sit children on their laps in shopping centres and give them gifts, have become highly commercialised figures. St Nicholas helps children to prepare inwardly for Christmas, rather than bringing material gifts (see also p. 42).

*Bishop Nicholas*

Here is a little story we tell the children in the days leading up to
December 6:

> Far away in the East lived a kind man, Bishop Nicholas.
> One day he heard that a long, long way away in the West
> was a big city where all the people went hungry, even
> the little children. He called his servants, who loved
> him, and said to them, 'Please bring me food from your
> fields and gardens so that we can feed these hungry
> people.' The servants brought large baskets filled with
> apples, and nuts from the trees in their gardens, and
> sacks containing golden grains from their fields. And
> the mothers sent gingerbread which they had baked
> themselves.
>
> Bishop Nicholas had all these gifts loaded on board a
> ship. It was a fine, big ship, as blue as the sky, and as blue
> as the bishop's cloak, and its white sails shone brightly in
> the sun.
>
> The wind blew in the sails, and whenever it grew tired
> of blowing, the servants took the oars and rowed the ship
> onwards. They had to journey for a long time: seven days
> and seven nights. When they arrived at the big city it was
> evening and there was no one in the streets, although
> light glinted from the windows.
>
> Bishop Nicholas knocked on a window. Inside a
> mother thought it was a late wanderer looking for
> shelter, and told her child to open the door. But no one
> was standing there. The child ran to the window but
> could see no one there either. But a basket stood there,
> and inside it there were yellow and red apples, and nuts,
> and on top some gingerbread. And next to it was a basket
> filled with golden grain. They took all of this into the
> house and the whole family sat down to eat. Soon the
> children grew healthy, and strong and happy again.

Now St Nicholas is in heaven. Every year, on his
birthday, he sets out on the path down to earth. He
mounts his white horse and travels from star to star.
There he meets Mother Mary as she gathers gold and
silver threads for the baby Jesus's little shirt. And she
says to Nicholas, 'Go down to the children once more,
take them your gifts and tell them that Christmas is
approaching and Jesus will soon be there.'

## Children at transition age – from wonder to guessing

Sooner or later in every child's life the moment arrives when
he starts to become aware of certain 'secrets' connected with St
Nicholas or Father Christmas (or the Christ Child in Germany).[11]
To avoid this leading to sudden disillusionment or loss of trust,
we try to accompany children at this age with particular attention
and inner solidarity.

Through imitation, children first learn to wonder. It does
not occur to them to question or doubt. Given up to all that is
deserving of wonder, they feel safe and secure in the adult's sure
guidance. Between the ages of five and seven, or even a little
later, it first begins to dawn on them that certain events involve
secrets. Older or more 'informed' children will often stimulate
this awakening. Some children can keep these questions to
themselves for a while, and become very alert observers. But most
children ask an adult about it, often in a reticent, even shy kind
of way.

I often find that a child will draw me into a quiet corner and
ask in a whisper whether it's true that St Nicholas was a man
dressed up. My first answer is frequently, 'Do you know, we
always tell each other such secrets very quietly.' Sometimes the
child will then run off happily. But if they stay to hear more,
I go on, 'Only very special people may wear the St Nicholas
cloak, carry the golden book and bring gifts to the children.'
The actual words one chooses are not so important, but

children should feel that these are mysterious things that need to be protected.

Seen in this light, we never need to confront children with untruths that later have to be cleared up. Rather, the nourishment needed by the developing human soul is offered at each stage in the appropriate form, as foundation for the subsequent health of the psyche.

Another little conversation shows how, at this time of transition, children above all want to show adults that they are aware of something. A six-year-old boy once asked me after I had set up the scene for the three kings, 'Why did you put wooden blocks like that under the cloth?' I replied, 'It has to be done like that', at which he went off very satisfied. He had let me know that he now 'saw through' everything.

Sometimes we may succeed in finding answers that retain their depth and significance right into later life, and we can feel the grace of such moments. A six-and-a-half-year-old girl once asked me about the basket of secrets brought by St Nicholas: 'Do you do that, or is it really St Nicholas's helpers?' I replied, 'It really is the helpers. All grown-ups can be helpers, and all children can eventually become helpers too.'[12]

We can respond in a similar way to questions about Father Christmas. What is important is that children feel our inner certainty; that they are allowed to live for a while with these true pictures; that in the early years of school they can widen their souls through a wealth of truth-imbued images in the form of stories; and that as adolescents and adults they become able to penetrate the profound content of these images with their conscious thinking.

## *Advent activities*

We have already spoken about setting up and caring for little moss gardens (see p. 33), which involves ongoing activity through Advent. Below we will look at further activities that are especially suitable for the Advent period.

### Candle dipping

We make our own candles for the moss gardens. To do so, we collect wax residues throughout the year, which are first melted down and then made into new candles by repeatedly dipping a thread wick into the hot wax. This process requires much patience and persistence, which most children manage to find in the calming atmosphere and lovely aroma of beeswax. Some children always want to make several candles, which we then use for the crib scene on the seasonal nature table. The important thing is to ensure that the preparations have been carefully thought through and are carried out calmly, with all the safety precautions necessary for hot water and hot wax. The children sit around a sturdy packing case with newspaper on their knees, and after each dip and each new layer their wonder and joy increases at the growing candle. Detailed instructions for candle dipping can be found in *The Christmas Craft Book*. [13]

### Candle holders

To ensure that the candles have a secure base, we give children small, soft balls of clay into which they press their candle. By moulding the holder a little around the candle, an individual holder is formed. We make sure that the base surface stays flat, and into the base we etch the name of each child with a sharpened pencil point, so that later the children will get their own candles back.

### Transparencies

It is easy to make simple transparent pictures from coloured tissue paper and a cardboard frame. While the children are having free play, an adult can make transparencies, setting up a worktable so that all the children – of whatever age – can join in if they wish. For instance, if we put off-cuts of gold cardboard and coloured tissue paper in the children's basket, to which they have free access, and place a small dish of water-soluble glue within reach, the children can plunge enthusiastically into this creative activity.

Like the adult, the children will repeatedly hold their coloured paper collages up to the light, and take pleasure in their luminosity and the creation of new colour tones. Only a few particularly skilled six-year-olds are likely to try creating a recognisable figure or shape, as they see the adult doing.

The valuable thing about this activity is that, again unconsciously, the children experience how we can render something transparent, to encompass the light that is seeking to reveal itself anew during Christmas. This is similar to the adult's efforts to prepare inwardly for Christmas (as described on p. 19). You will find full instructions on making a range of transparencies in *The Christmas Craft Book*. [14]

*Making small gifts*

Apart from the things we have mentioned – a small moss garden, dipping candles, making simple transparencies – some children come up with other ideas for gifts for their loved ones. They are very good at knowing their own capacities, and we should let them make things freely and happily, just offering a little help now and then if they ask for it. The desire to make something often comes from imitation, particularly when they're surrounded by a cheerful atmosphere of industrious activity. For instance, after the candle holders containing the self-dipped candles have been wrapped in fine tissue paper, tied with little ribbons and inscribed with the children's names, there are always boxes left over containing used gift-wrapping paper. Sometimes this inspires children to make a little gift, for which they carefully choose a suitable piece of wrapping paper. Such gifts might be a needle-book or pin-cushion made of felt; a small, self-bound picture book with painted pictures; a little wallet, maybe even with a button; a letter opener carved by an adult from a thin, narrow slat which the child can sand smooth; or gold stars cut out freehand. The important thing is not to impose expectations on pre-school children but to let them set to work out of their own impulse, stimulated by older siblings or adults.

*The Christmas play*

Immediately after the feast of St Nicholas, clothes and veils for the Christmas play are lying ready. The play is composed of Christmas songs and only a very few spoken lines, and its preparation informs much of what happens in the next two weeks of Advent until the end of term. During their free play time, the children dress up repeatedly in the clothes and act out the little play for themselves. Their preparations – dressing up and setting up the crib – usually take a good deal longer than the play itself.

At the end of the morning we all act the play together. The chairs are placed in position and each day the children put on a different outfit. This is not a rehearsed play in which each person is responsible for a role, but is performed entirely through imitation. In other words, the adult sings and says everything, goes through the whole story and does all the gestures. The children follow and imitate, grasping each scene more or less consciously according to their age.

In various kindergartens the Christmas play is also performed as a ring game, in which all the children take on all the 'roles' together. This means that throughout the play they keep moving in a circle, or around the teacher, and this has proven to be good especially in groups with mainly young children.

The play described above starts, instead, from a tableau that is easy for the children to take in, and at the same time involves a developing process. Having an opportunity to put on the various different clothes, especially Mary's dress, is for some children not just beneficial but even healing.

## Christmas in kindergarten

The concluding festival of Advent in the kindergarten, to which parents are usually invited, will probably vary as much as the way each family celebrates Christmas. Thus the ideas for this festival suggested below should really only be taken as stimulus for creating your own distinct celebration.

In preparatory discussions with parents we always try to think of ways in which, despite being an audience for once, they can still be actively involved. The children very much look forward to their parents coming to our small Christmas play and helping us with singing and lyre playing. On two evenings during Advent, a few parents learn to play the children's harp, and their children see them practising the songs at home.

At the Christmas festival, the instruments and the quiet, communal singing create a lovely atmosphere.

A quite different kind of help that parents can offer involves them trying, during the play, to look at the whole scene rather than catching their own child's eye. This can pull children out of their often hard-won connection with what is unfolding.

*The festival day*

Once the children are dressed up in their costumes and sitting on their chairs, and have fallen quiet, their parents come in and sit down around them in a large semi-circle. The parents with the children's harps sit down by the music stands, and after a few words of greeting, the children perform the play in the way they have been used to doing (see p. 50).

After the play, there are a few transitional moments – which must have been well prepared and thought through to avoid things getting too loud or chaotic – for children to take off the costumes and for chairs to be rearranged. Natural chatting and conversation is fine at this point, and even necessary, so that children are not kept quiet for too long. Then the children sit down in a semi-circle in front of their parents in such a way that everyone can look at the big nativity scene on the nature table, where the candles are now lit.

Before the crib scene stands a large candle, and to the left and right two vases containing fir branches. Some kindergartens include a lily in one and a red rose in the other.

Now follows a more convivial time when we eat the Christmas biscuits that have been specially baked for today. Then each child receives a candle apple that they may light from the big candle, one after another. As they do so we sing Christmas songs. Again, during this process, the children experience how everything grows slowly brighter through this shared activity. Once all the candles are lit (for safety precautions, see p. 38) , and after singing our loveliest Christmas song I tell the children in farewell that soon Christmas will come, and then their home will be bright with candlelight. After thanking the parents, and offering good wishes for a lovely Christmas, the kindergarten teacher goes from one child to another putting out each candle with a snuffer.

In some kindergartens, the candles are placed in the children's moss gardens instead, and lit there. Afterwards, the children carry their little garden, with lit candle, to their parents. This symbolic act is also connected with the wonderful idea that adults can find their own spiritual light through the forces of childhood (see also Matthew 18:3, 'Except ye become as little children...').

Another way of celebrating the Christmas festival is to follow the Christmas play with a convivial feast of Christmas biscuits at festively decorated tables or in a large circle, and end with the singing of Christmas songs.

## Christmas at home

In Germany the main Christmas celebrations are traditionally held on Christmas Eve, whereas in many other Western countries they are celebrated on December 25, Christmas Day. The following advice can be adapted to suit your preference.

### Preparation

After all the preparation and busy activity, Christmas Eve is a culmination. But special efforts are needed to ensure that it represents a fulfilment for all involved. These efforts relate both to outward preparations, primarily decoration, and also to a carefully planned sequence for the evening. First of all, of course, the Advent room must be turned into a Christmas room. Where circumstances allow, perhaps this room could have been closed since the previous evening and throughout the day; a star hung up on the door can testify to secret things going on behind it, which children may try to glimpse through the keyhole or hear by putting their ears to the door.

*The Christmas tree*

The Christmas tree has a special place in our culture. Until only a few decades ago, many families in Germany brought the tree indoors secretly, without children present. A little scene from kindergarten in the sixties can give a sense of this:

> On a warm September morning the children were playing in the garden. I sat down on a log for a moment to rest from gardening work when a small group of four-year-olds appeared, hauling bits of tree trunk, and placed them before me without a word of explanation. Then, with outspread, winging arms, they ran off to get more logs. When they came back again the third time, and I still didn't know what they were up to, I said, 'Thank you very much.' At this they protested loudly and said, 'No, you can't see us, we're the angels, and we're bringing you Christmas trees.'

Today, when you can see Christmas trees being sold all over the place and children – since there's no other way to do it – are often there when a tree is chosen, at least the tree can be decorated secretly. Its most important decoration, alongside all other individual preferences, are its lights.

*The nativity scene*

It's lovely for children if the crib scene, with figures as described in the Gospel of St Luke, can be set up under the Christmas tree on

Christmas Eve: the stable with Mary, Joseph and the child, the ox and ass, and the shepherds. An angel can stand there too.

If a slowly growing nativity scene has been present through Advent, there are various ways in which the manger and baby Jesus can appear on Christmas Day or Eve. The important thing is for the tableau to culminate in the arrival of the long-awaited child in the manger.

*Getting children in the right mood*

A mysterious day such as this, when the last preparations are being made, may not be very easy for children. Naturally there is a growing expectancy and anticipation, and it may help to lead this into a purposeful activity. For instance, a friend of the family might relieve the parents for a while by filling empty walnut shells, with a loop attached, with fat and sunflower seeds as Christmas presents for the birds. Or a basket full of collected acorns and conkers might stand ready, for taking to the forest on a walk and scattering for the wild animals.

It's lovely for children if they can experience the stillness of a wood or meadow on this day, and be fully engaged in their own activity of giving. City children who have no forest nearby will no doubt be able to find little trees or bushes in a park or front garden where they can hang up gifts for the birds. (In kindergarten we tend to do this in the last few days before the Christmas holidays.) If the day is fine, luminous colours will appear at twilight, and soon afterwards the first star.

*Christmas presents*

In many families, presents are placed to the left and right of the nativity scene under the Christmas tree. Or equally, a certain place in the Christmas room can be set up for each person, to which they are led to find their gifts.

To encourage children to unwrap their presents carefully, these should *not* be sealed with adhesive tape – as this makes it tempting to rip the present open. It's good if wrapping paper can be carefully folded and stored in a box for later use. Nor, for ease of opening, should ribbons around presents be double-knotted, which may require hard tugging or even scissors.

Some presents may perhaps be placed ready without paper wrapping, but instead be covered with a cloth so as not to distract children when the celebration begins.

It's significant for children if they can perceive our inner stance when, for instance, we wrap up a little parcel for loved ones, perhaps the child's godparents or grandparents. Children have a direct experience, deeper than our words, of the thoughts and feelings we invest in our actions. Simply seeing lovely wrapping paper, ribbons, Christmas cards and so forth can kindle an atmosphere that spurs children to activity. The younger ones may wrap up some small treasure, and then also unwrap it again to see what it was they wrapped up. Very small ones can draw something for a relative, even if this is still a 'scribble'. Soon a need will develop to make something as a gift. Children who have learned to give from a young age, and who have also learned to receive with gratitude, do not suffer the abrupt shock of being 'enlightened' when they find out that Father Christmas doesn't exist. It's also helpful in this regard, and truthful, if not all gifts are said to come from Father Christmas – certainly not the ones that arrive by post!

*Celebrating Christmas Eve (or Day)*

Returning home from a walk to the warm house, we can change and put on festive clothes; and then wait in a room lit by only one candle until a little bell or musical instrument announces the moment when the door is opened to reveal the illumined Christmas tree. As we gaze in wonder at the tree and the nativity scene, songs – best of all ones that family members sing themselves – resound, and if possible also instruments.

In many families the Christmas story is read from Luke, Chapter 2, and even the youngest children can share in this, sitting on a parent's lap. This can be followed by a little recorder piece, or a beautiful verse, or a simple, self-devised Christmas play, performed by older siblings who go to school already, perhaps with the help of the parents.

After this little celebration it is time for the giving of presents, or this may take place the following day. For children this is a further sign of fulfilment, with jubilation at their own gifts and those given to the others.

Besides the Christmas treats that are nibbled now, at some point of course there will also be a festive (though maybe modest) meal at a beautifully laid table. Or you may want to have a more festive meal on Christmas Day, and just a hearty supper on Christmas Eve, perhaps prepared together by everyone earlier in the day to take the pressure off busy adults.

However different Christmas Eve and Day may be in each household, and whatever traditions you like to uphold, all the preparations, the festive decorations, the aroma of fir branches, candles and baking, the words and live music and the unwrapping of presents will all set the right mood for the Christmas festival of light and love. Such impressions will go deep into the child's soul and nurture sustaining forces that work on into later life.

The real fulfilment of Christmas can scarcely be described in words. The light of Jesus is surely what fills and fulfils our hearts, and seeks to stream through us into the world. With Jesus, humanity receives the gift of new light and love. However, we can have a clear sense of the effort we need to make to receive this gift of love and light.

Children cannot understand this intellectually but they sense it. Rudolf Steiner was concerned that young children should not be confronted with abstract religious concepts and explanations. But they should hear the *name* of Jesus, already in the cradle, resounding from an adult's heart in a song or prayer. What counts is the way we speak to a one-, two-, three- or four-year-old child. Our words should arise from a living contact with the child, and from true feelings. Trying to find the right content and words for each age, so that we really speak to the child, is an endeavour that offers huge challenges and scope for development for us as educators. Here we participate in the foundations of human culture, which are created in the earliest years.

# The Twelve Holy Nights and Epiphany

## *Creating the mood ourselves*

During the twelve Holy Nights that follow Christmas, the events of Christmas continue to resonate; and it is a lovely custom for children if candles are lit each day, with singing, music making and perhaps a reading. This period is set apart from the rest of the year, and can be a time when we gather our strength for the year ahead. Nothing urgent needs to be done, and we can really take time for things. Children are deeply satisfied if a parent or carer sits down beside them with some craftwork, or perhaps joins in a game now and then. In contrast to the summer when we like going outdoors, we feel very comfortable at home in the warmth – apart from winter walks and the fun of snow when it comes.

The mood that we now try to create in ourselves can receive further impetus from the following lines by Friedrich Hebbel:

> And down from all the stars
> Streams blessing like wondrous rain
> So that all our weary powers
> Grow newly fresh again.
>
> And out of obscure dark
> The Lord comes into view
> To knit torn threads together
> And all of life renew.

In the last few days of December, the shepherds in the nativity scene make their way homewards again. At the beginning of the new year, therefore, we can transform the scene and now introduce the kings. Ideas for the new tableau can be found in the Gospel of St Matthew, and also by carefully observing and comparing artistic depictions of the worshipping shepherds on the one hand, and the adoration of the magi on the other. Whereas the Gospel of St Luke tells of the birth in a stable, to which the shepherds come, Matthew speaks of the birth in a house, attended by three wise men from the East.

The kings saw the star that had newly appeared, revealing its special light to them and announcing the arrival of the son of God on earth. The forthcoming event was so mighty that they set off from distant lands to give it a fitting welcome, and to bring their offerings. Melchior, the red king, offers gold as a symbol of wisdom; Balthasar, the blue king, offers frankincense, a symbol of piety; and Caspar, the green king, offers myrrh as a symbol of vitality, healing and will forces.

## Epiphany with children

### The seasonal nature table

In kindergarten, the holidays make it easy to transform the tableau on the nature table from the landscape of the shepherds to that of the kings. For the adoration of the kings we take our lead from the Gospel of St Matthew: instead of a natural scene with moss, we lay down a covering cloth of light blue, upon which lovely crystals are placed.

The stable is replaced by a house or a background formed of round pieces of wood, perhaps covered with veils of golden yellow and bright yellow. Behind this can stand a vase containing delicate branches of silver pine to which a bright star is attached. In many old pictures we find an eight-pointed star depicted in connection with the kings. Mary now has the child sitting upright in her lap: he can be dressed in white and wear a golden halo.

Led by the angel, the kings approach a little nearer each day.

The angel's star wand can now hold a star which shows an image of the virgin with child. Once the kings have brought their gifts at Epiphany, they slowly make their way back again. Then, during the last days of January, Mary, sitting with the child upon the donkey, and Joseph leading it, travel 'into Egypt'.

If a child ever asks why Mary and Joseph are going to Egypt, I always reply, 'Because the angel told them to.' This has always proven an entirely satisfactory reply for them, since it has been spoken out of a conviction that the actions of Herod do not yet have to find their way directly into the pre-school child's experience.

*The three kings play*

The events of the three kings' story are once again grasped actively in the form of a little play. We try to keep acting it out until the fourth week in January, or even up to Candlemas day on February 2.

It is naturally not possible for the children to sustain the role of a king, therefore the story unfolds entirely through imitation. All the children, even the younger ones, are very keen to be a king, as though they can already sense their own future in this role. All of us, after all, are on the path towards our inner kingship. Goethe once put it like this:

After an event has happened
We can hear it still much later:
Once the bell's been struck it keeps
Reverberating on forever.
Let these tones ring on in us
Brightening our hearts and souls;
For in the end we surely all
Are kings progressing to our goals.

*Johann Wolfgang Goethe*

## *Looking back*

If we review the whole Christmas period again, with its weeks of preparation and the time of Epiphany or the three kings, we find it covers a span of twice forty days. From the earliest possible date of Advent Sunday on November 27 through to January 6 there are forty days; and likewise forty days from December 24 to February 2 (Candlemas). Where these two spans overlap we have the twelve Holy Nights, whose beginning we celebrate on December 24 with the birth of Jesus.

Epiphany, January 6, is also the date of the Jordan baptism, when the heavens opened and the Holy Spirit entered Jesus. This event, which we can see as the true birth of Christ, was celebrated as the Christmas festival until the fourth century. Only subsequently did the feast of the child's birth acquire its special importance, and was brought forward to December 25, the day following Adam and Eve day.

We never speak to children about these mysterious connections, but we try ourselves to penetrate them increasingly with the help of anthroposophy. Thus the insights we gain can live in our inner life and feed unspoken into the way we celebrate festivals with children.

After Epiphany we only keep a few crystals on the nature table, on the light blue cloth. Depending on weather conditions, a wintry mood may still prevail, which we can indicate with a delicate white veil. Sunlight now starts to increase, sap starts rising in the trees – and so the crystals are soon replaced by the first heralds of early spring, in the form of bare twigs and snowdrops. Under its pointed hat, the hyacinth now starts to poke out, giving us just a glimpse of its colourful dress.

During this time falls the cheerful bustle of Carnival, and in the next section we will look at some possible ways of celebrating this with kindergarten children.

# Carnival

Carnival is celebrated immediately before Lent, as a final burst of exuberance before the traditional forty days of fasting. Carnival is a popular festival in the Catholic tradition, and combines public parades and dressing up. Shrove Tuesday (Pancake Day) is a version of the same principle, when we use up our rich food in preparation for Lent. In Steiner schools in English-speaking countries, the Carnival festival is often held on Shrove Tuesday.

## Preparation with children

The need of adults to slip into another 'skin' once a year, in order to identify wholly with a different creature or person, is one that pre-school children satisfy every day while playing. In quick succession, often within only a few minutes, they can change from being one thing to another, and arrange their games accordingly. Young children take great pleasure in uniting through imitation with all visible processes in their surroundings, especially with activities carried out by people. From this perspective we don't really need Carnival for little ones. If we do celebrate it, it is in order to reflect in the children's immediate environment, in a way they can relate to, what is already living and unfolding around them.

Of all the diverse possibilities for a theme, I would suggest the following: crafts and professions, gnomes, fairy tales, a king and queen's castle, and mermaids. In our kindergarten we always choose crafts and professions, which is a wide-ranging theme and offers all sorts of related activities. This will be described in more detail here, since we have most experience with it.

In the days beforehand, we and the children clear the whole classroom and use parasols and stands to build different workplaces for: bakers, fishermen, shoemakers, carpenters, painters and parents (of course other trades and tasks could be chosen too).

We also make tiny rolls, loaves, sweet pastries and other things from a quark-flour dough. For the fishermen, apart from colourful beeswax fish with a ring for catching, we make little fish from fruit-jelly sweets wrapped in silver foil, with tiny clamps attached for catching. For the carpenters' and shoemakers' workshops we fetch tree-stump stools from the garden for sitting or hammering on. For the painters we hang up three layers of newspaper on a wall. We don't mix the colours until Carnival day itself, stirring them with wallpaper paste to avoid too much dripping. The dolls are laid in cribs for the mothers to care for. On the day before Carnival, we decorate the 'houses' a little with coloured crêpe-paper and lay out all the tools and materials.

The children help eagerly with all these preparations. Many also go into the workshops already and start playing imaginatively there. For instance, the bakers sell loaves made of bits of bark, and biscuits made of small slices of wood and conkers. The fishermen make themselves big lakes everywhere on the ground (but only fish for the wax fish). The carpenter's hammer with building blocks, not yet using proper nails. The parents sometimes decorate their 'windowsill' (play stand) with 'pot plants' made of thick, round pieces of wood with a thin, scrunched-up cloth on top. In a far corner they may use benches and fabrics to arrange a comfortable little sleeping chamber.

## Carnival day

In the morning, at the usual time, the children arrive at kindergarten already dressed up. The 'costume' may just be hinted at, perhaps with a white apron and baker's hat, fisherman's overalls and hat, painter's overalls, carpenter's apron, and outfits for the parents. We agree with the children's actual parents to avoid make-up. During free play, busy, peaceful activity prevails everywhere. The bakers brush their loaves with white and brown icing sugar, spread butter on the halved rolls for our morning snack, and decorate them with raisins. The fishermen rejoice each time they catch a fish. In the wood workshop there's banging and sawing. The painters are usually quietly immersed in their work. The parents lay the table, dress their doll children and go for walks with them. Of course any child can go and work anywhere, irrespective of their costume – there are always plenty of tools and materials. And the children cannot yet, and should not be, asked to 'maintain a role'. From time to time the bakers' bell rings, and then everyone comes to buy bread from them.

On this morning the kindergarten teacher goes from house to house and just makes sure all is well.

After the free-play period, the parents arrive while all the children are in the washroom. They are not wearing costumes. Some crouch down in front of their children, each of whom wraps a streamer many times round their neck. Now they are dressed up for Carnival too. In a long line we go into the classroom singing. The house stands have been pushed back a little to make as much space as possible for a 'market place'. Here we do our dances and craftsmen plays together. The 'fishing lake game' is the highpoint, in which all children are fishes and the parents form the net together.

For the festive morning snack, the parents go with their children into the workshops. This is rather squashed, but very cosy.

Afterwards – if there's enough space – we play Bird Mother, which is a hiding game. All the children are the birds in a nest. When the Bird Mother (parents) fall asleep, squatting, all the birds fly away to hide. The teacher helps a little. Each Bird Mother may then only find her own child, and must otherwise cover up the hiding place again quickly. Once all the little birds have been found, we swap roles, and the parents hide. In choosing a hiding place they naturally take account of the child's age.

We conclude our cheerful activities with a big ring game together, and a dance involving everyone.

# Spring

Winter slowly fades, taking with it the dark and cold, and the structuring forces apparent right into the crystalline patterns of snowflakes. Spring approaches, and with it nature starts to awaken: plant saps begin to flow, light increases and the first rays of warmth stream back. Everywhere new life starts to reveal itself. Buds swell on the trees and bushes, the first snowdrops, winter aconite, coltsfoot and crocuses open to the sunlight, and the air fills with subtle scents. Animals wake from hibernation; flocks of birds return and their twittering fills the air. Children also want to get out into the open air again, and each day brings new discoveries.

When weather conditions allow, we uncover the garden beds where tulips and daffodils are poking out their first green tips. A suitable song such as, 'Mother Earth, Mother Earth'[16] resounds frequently, with its story, which we sing and play as a ring game, of seeds waking up in sunshine, wind and rain:

Mother Earth,
Mother Earth,
Take our seed
And give it birth.

Sister Rain,
Sister Rain,
Shed thy tears
To swell the grain.

Father Sun,
Gleam and glow,
Until the roots
Begin to grow.

Brother Wind,
Breathe and blow
Then the blade
Green will grow.

Earth and Sun,
And wind and rain,
Turn to gold
The living grain.

*Eileen Hutchins*


You will find many songs, poems and stories which help
sustain the spring mood. This one is popular in our kindergarten:

Dwight the gnome pulled on a bulb
in the forest where he lived
and from it sprang a little blue
blossom welcoming the spring.
Dwight the gnome called to the hare
in his mossy hidey-hole:
'Hurry, run and tell them all
my little flower is blossoming.'
And the lark high in the heavens
and the mole in the dark tunnel
and the deer deep in the forest
all come flying, creeping, running
to see the little blossom unfold
its lovely blue and welcome spring.[17]

Children in cities can also experience spring's awakening if
they are taken for regular walks in parks, and allowed to dwell
a little on what they find. Every glittering pebble, the ants that
rush away with their eggs, the many plane or maple seedlings
that suddenly start germinating, will bring joy to children's
hearts if adults surround them with their own lively and loving
awareness of nature. And if you catch sight of a small snail
slowly creeping along, a little verse like the following may
spring to mind.

Slowly, slowly, very slowly
Creeps the garden snail.
Slowly, slowly, very slowly
Up the wooden rail.

Quickly, quickly, very quickly
Runs the little mouse.
Quickly, quickly, very quickly
Round about the house.

We can also bring something of this spring mood into the house by gathering things for the seasonal nature table (see p. 11). It is now covered in a green cloth which can be partly covered in turn by a delicate pink veil. Upon this stands a large vase containing budding twigs, and small vases holding the first spring flowers. Here too is a fitting place for things the children have brought, such as empty snail shells. Nearer Easter, the basket in which we collect blown eggs can stand on the table as well.

In the ten to fourteen days before the Easter holidays we have our big spring clean. After the long winter, and with an eye to the forthcoming festival, this busy cleaning activity is one of vigorous renewal, and children take part in it enthusiastically. If warm spring days have arrived, some of this cleaning can take place outdoors. What a lovely fresh smell the laundry has when it can flutter and dry in the spring wind.

Before the Easter holidays begin, in some kindergartens the children paint a blown egg. In Germany these eggs are put in a basket and covered over for Easter. In doing this the children can see what's coming but at the same time learn that we have to wait for the right moment. Later, after the holidays, these eggs will be hanging on the Easter tree. However, in many countries, such as the UK, Easter is celebrated in kindergarten before the holidays.

# Easter

## *Creating the mood ourselves*

After the spring equinox on March 21, the sun progresses victoriously, its daily arcs expanding and rising ever higher. The Easter festival is celebrated on the Sunday following the spring full moon, at the beginning of the time when days are growing longer.

The core Easter theme is 'death and resurrection', towards a deeper understanding of which the child's soul can only slowly mature. Children are continually surrounded by processes of flourishing and dying, and during the school years, from around age six onwards, they start to become increasingly aware of these.

Every death already contains the seed of new life, as nature shows us in the most diverse ways. New leaf buds form in autumn as the old leaves are shed and life forces withdraw. Ripe fruits can serve as food, or also wither and rot; they contain the new seed from which a seedling will sprout as soon as the right conditions prevail. In the animal kingdom we can recall the caterpillar that weaves its cocoon, pupates in darkness and then emerges transformed as a butterfly. In the ancient mysteries this natural occurrence was already seen as an image of the human soul's immortality; and Goethe's *Faust* ends with the words, 'Everything transient is but a metaphor.'[18]

The mighty, transformational event that occurred, uniquely, 2,000 years ago at Golgotha on behalf of humanity, is not easily accessible to us today. We have to make conscious efforts if we are really to absorb the mystery of the resurrected God. Anthroposophy, conveyed by Rudolf Steiner in a way appropriate to our modern consciousness, is an aid to us here.[19] In many of

Steiner's lectures on the festivals, the Mystery of Golgotha has key importance. We can try to take these great events into our soul and deepen them year on year, which will strengthen the relationship to our work with children during Easter, and also for all other Christian festivals. For young children who connect with everything through their senses, it's important that we succeed in imbuing our actions and gestures with what lives in our thoughts and feelings, leading children to an experience, rather than just an explanation, of natural processes. This creates a sound foundation which can later help them to consciously grasp the greatest mysteries and interconnections.

## Preparing for Easter

### The Easter garden

One of the most evident and telling images of the transformations of death and resurrection can be found in the seed. It is therefore a wonderful, meaningful activity to sow seeds with children in the pre-Easter period. It is important for adults to prepare themselves inwardly for the special moment of sowing the evening before, so that their gestures are informed in the right way. In order for the children to experience this task deeply, as suggested above, everything depends on the inner stance with which we approach this cheerful and busy activity. The time for sowing will depend a little on the type of seed. Spring wheat grows 5–7 cm (2–3 in) in a week, whereas grass needs a little longer, but no more than two weeks. The time it takes not only depends on the type of grass seed but also on the garden's location, and the warmth and humidity.

Firstly we fetch earth from outside and break it up with our fingers to form a fine tilth, removing all little stones and bits of twig. And if we find an earthworm, beetle or centipede, we naturally return it to the flowerbeds. Some of the earth is sieved very finely in a second bucket. If it is sunny spring weather, this work can be done outdoors, or otherwise inside on well-covered tables.

The next day we fill the clay pots which the children have brought in for this purpose – first with the broken-up earth and then with a layer of the sieved earth on top, firming it down a little by hand. Now the kindergarten teacher and children start to sow the seeds, while singing the traditional song, 'Oats and beans and barley grow' or saying a verse such as this:

We're sowing, we're sowing the small seeds so fine
we sprinkle them into the earth one by one,
we cover them over
and now let them slumber.

And soon a green tip
will poke its way up:
little shoots will appear
and we'll water them there.
And as we tend our garden, so
lovely Easter grass will grow.

After *H. Diestel*

Some children – still rather dreamily – will only put their seeds in the middle of the pot to begin with, while others will not rest until the whole surface is covered and scarcely any earth can be seen. The kindergarten teacher helps them. Then, with a little fine soil, we cover over the seeds and 'now let them slumber'.

Before placing the little gardens on a windowsill, we 'let it rain' by watering the bowls carefully using a fine sprinkler or watering can. Filling the bowls and sowing takes the whole of free-play time. Some children break up the earth more and more finely before they go over to the teacher and start sowing. Each can pursue this activity in peace, in their own time. There are always a few children gathered round the teacher while others are playing. If the gardens are kept moist, after three to five days the first green tips will poke out, and the children will start to get excited, almost urging the shoots out of the earth with their glances.

On the last day of term before the Easter holidays, the children take their gardens home and leave them ready for the Easter hare – either outdoors, or on a balcony, or in the house, depending on weather and circumstances.

After Easter it is important to give the gardens back to nature and not simply throw them out with the rubbish. We therefore plant them by the edge of a meadow or in a park.

During this time, too, children will often make little Easter nests out of moss or pine needles in the garden or wherever they stop on walks, and put pebbles, snail shells, fir cones and suchlike inside.

## The Easter hare

In relation to Easter, the hare offers us an image of the selflessness exemplified by the figure of Christ. In old legends and tales it is said that the hare is willing to sacrifice itself for other creatures. Something similar has been witnessed in hare hunts when hares have appeared willing to take the place of another, exhausted hare and thus selflessly sacrifice themselves. Of course this is done quite instinctively, and cannot be based, as with human beings, on a conscious decision.

The hare is also an animal that never injures another, but is itself continually pursued and harried by others. With its long, sensitive ears, it must stay alert to its surroundings, and its only means of escaping pursuit is to run faster or change direction suddenly. For this reason it is connected with the moon, which hastens across the sky more swiftly than any planet.

When, on walks with children, we see a hare leaping across a field, and the children say, 'Look, there's the Easter hare,' there's no need to contradict them. But if a child asks, 'Is that the Easter hare?' we can reply that it's his friend and helper, and that the Easter hare is surely somewhere close by. A close companion to the spring goddess Ostara, the Easter hare is invisible to us. On Easter morning he brings and hides bright, colourful eggs, awaking our seeking impulse.

But what does the hare have to do with the egg? We will return to this question below, in connection with the Easter egg.

## Easter eggs

The egg is the germ of new life and development, in contrast to the fruit which we celebrate in autumn, which marks the close and culmination of development. In ancient mythologies, such as the Finnish epic *Kalevala*, the world is created out of an egg, the upper half of the shell becoming the heavens, the lower half the earth, the yolk turning into the sun and the white of the egg the moon.

At the same time, the egg is an image of the eternal, immortal or imperishable core of the human being. Ancient peoples expressed this by placing an egg into the grave of their dead. They knew that death only means transformation, and that it marks the beginning of a new life for the soul. There was also a custom in which friends visiting after the birth of a child would place an egg in the cradle. This was done to show that here, too, a transformation had occurred, and a new life had begun. In his *Fragments*, Novalis writes, 'When a human dies he becomes spirit. When a spirit dies he becomes human.'

The egg as an image of origin and beginning was adopted by Christianity and connected with the greatest new beginning in humanity's history, when Christ united with the man Jesus of Nazareth at the Jordan baptism. As a lofty divine being, he suffered death in a human body, but he overcame death, and from then on can be sought and found by each of us.

We see that the egg acquires great significance as a metaphor of nature's awakening in spring and of the new beginning wrested from death at Easter.

The Easter egg, though, is no ordinary egg, for here a natural product from the animal kingdom is enhanced by human efforts. With all our individual artistic and creative capacities, we can endow the egg with colours and shapes. By choosing some kind of ordered, ornamental pattern for this, or by freely arranging the colours in a harmonious way, we can follow cosmic principles; for the cosmos signifies order and harmony and stands in contrast to mere caprice or chaos. In eastern countries, particularly, one can still find wonderful, artistic examples of this. Using bright, luminous colours and a wealth of forms and shapes, we can express all our joy and rejoicing at the new beginning in nature and the resurrection of Christ.

*Painting eggs with children*

Painting blown eggs with children requires great care. It's best if the children sit at tables for this. We use normal wax blocks (Stockmar), and the luminosity and coverage the children can achieve with these are astonishing. Adults always try to create lovely colour gradations, ordered patterns and shapes; and older children over five, especially, will try to copy the adults. They often spend a long time decorating their egg, in rapt concentration. Naturally we never try to correct them but leave them completely free to imitate and create as they like. Once an egg is finished we place a small piece of matchstick into the larger blowing hole, with a thread attached for hanging. Of course eggs can also be painted with watercolours if you place them on a small support.

*Hare and egg*

Let's now consider how the hare is connected with the egg. We saw that the hare embodies a kind of natural selflessness and self-sacrifice. If we succeed in practising this consciously, we have embarked on the path of awakening Christ forces within us. On the road to Damascus, Paul experienced this encounter with Christ, and found himself able to say, 'Not I, but Christ in me' (Galatians 2:20). The egg can embody this connection with the eternal in us. And if we tell children about the Easter hare who brings the eggs, we connect a truthful and profound meaning with it.

## Seeking and finding

The Easter egg has further significance. We saw that the egg is a germ cell from which new life can unfold. But how this new beginning grows and develops is initially open. We often seek the right inner path, looking for meaning in life and listening to events of destiny in our own life and those of others. The hidden Easter egg reminds us of the need to invoke our will on this search.

Children love hunting and finding Easter eggs, with all the sensory immediacy this involves. We can observe that children only grasp the meaning of seeking and finding from a certain age. Very young children, at around the age of two, run happily through the garden, forest or house and, if they find an egg, can just sit beside it contentedly without immediately taking possession of it. This cheerful seeking and finding outdoors can be an expression of the inner effort we make as adults.

## Further Easter activities

### Larch- or pine-cone hares

Making simple hares can be a good activity in preparation for Easter, and can also stimulate children's play. We think it's best if children make them purely through imitation, on their own and without help. We take beautiful larch cones, into which small ash keys can be stuck to make ears, using a little glue if necessary. Some children make many at once, and use them in their games. For instance, they might build little hare burrows for them on the floor or the table, connected to each other by paths, then create a lovely landscape around this for the hares to spring about in. The same happens with hares and Easter lambs made of unspun

sheep's wool, which are described below. It is important that an adult repeatedly makes these hares and lambs over several days, at a specially allocated time, in order to create an atmosphere of activity which the children can imitate by finding sufficient materials in the 'children's basket'.[20]

*Hares and lambs from unspun sheep's wool*

First make an egg shape from loosely teased sheep's wool. Tie the head off using a drawn-out strand of wool in such a way that it does not hang downwards (see drawing overleaf). By pulling the thin neck-strand tight, an egg-shaped head is created. The ears are carefully pulled out from the head and shaped: in the case of the hare, into long upright or backward pointing ears; and in the case of the lamb, they can hang down by the side of the head. Pull the ears to a slight point between thumb and forefinger, and tease the wool out more broadly towards the head.

Place a little basket or a soft cloth ready to receive the finished hares or lambs.

*Easter candles*

Set a candle upright in a little soft wax in the middle of a shallow bowl or deep saucer. Lay a thick layer of moss all round the candle, and then, using a very thin twig or stick, make little holes in the moss where spring flowers can be placed. If there is sufficient water in the bowl, the flowers will stay fresh for many days. Children can make these Easter candles too, and they look lovely on the Easter breakfast table.

## Easter at home

How one celebrates Easter at home will depend largely on the family itself, and may well change and develop through time. Here I will just describe some customs that kindergarten-age children can share in.

We do not specifically mention to younger children the

matters which older children and adults may be concerned with at Passiontide, but they can certainly be involved in some of the pre-Easter preparations. On a walk they may find little flowers which they bring home to decorate Easter candles or the Easter table. They also love helping with the baking of Easter bread. And they participate with quiet anticipation and concentration in the painting of blown eggs, which will later decorate the Easter tree or table. The eggs, however, should not be hung up yet, but carefully placed in a basket and covered over with a cloth. All further preparations are now up to the adults.

When waking up on Easter morning, the cheerful and expectant mood can be further enhanced with an Easter song sung together, and perhaps a spoken Easter verse.

To everyone I say, he lives
has risen once again,
that he is there within our midst
to stay with us forever.
I tell each person, and each one
tells it to his friends in turn:
that soon and everywhere will dawn
the new kingdom of heaven.
He lives and now will be with us
when we are quite forsaken
and so this day may be a feast
of world rejuvenation.

*Novalis* [21]


It is good if the song is sung, or verse spoken, in front of the newly adorned seasonal nature table. The Easter tree or branch may stand there, with the coloured eggs now hanging from it, and a vase of daffodils and the Easter candle. If some of the children already go to 'big school', a picture of the risen Christ could hang on the wall behind the table – for instance the one by Matthias

Grünewald, or Fra Angelico's 'Noli me tangere'.

It may be that, before this, an adult has been on an early morning walk with the older children, perhaps climbing a hill where they waited for sunrise; or perhaps everyone has been out to fetch Easter water from a brook or spring. Either before breakfast or immediately afterwards, the children can rush out to hunt for Easter eggs. It is preferable that children only find eggs on their hunt, keeping the symbolism of this festival pure. Other occasions can be found for giving toys; it's best not to turn the Easter hare into Father Christmas or make Easter a festival of presents.

## Celebrating Easter in kindergarten

Because of the Easter holidays, we hold a small Easter celebration in kindergarten a week after Easter.[22] When the children return from the holidays, they can see that Easter has happened here too. On the seasonal nature table, with its green covering, stands a vase with branches from which bright, colourful eggs are hanging. But some white eggs are still in the basket, waiting to be turned into Easter eggs.

In some places, instead of an Easter tree, a wreath is made of boxwood branches, from which coloured eggs hang. Children enjoy helping to make this. Unlike the Advent wreath, this wreath can be formed of two rings intersecting at right angles.

On this first day of term all the preparations are for the actual festival the following day. We make a yeast dough and bake a large, round, braided loaf, in the middle of which is a cross. At the midpoint of the cross we place a raw egg that becomes hard-boiled during baking. This Easter bread embodies the picture of the cross and the beginning of new life, surrounded by the Easter sun. Apart from this big Easter loaf we also bake many small round loaves for the children to take home the next day. These small loaves are not braided but just rolled, and the children help make them. Naturally they also want to mark the central point, and for this we use a raisin.

In some kindergartens, Easter gnomes or human figures are baked, each holding an egg in their crossed arms – a picture of new life arising within the human being.

At the end of the morning we paint the many white eggs which we will use for decorations the following day.

Next day we push all the tables together to form a long, festive table, which we now slowly and peacefully decorate as beautifully as we can. Along the middle of the table lies a long, narrowly folded, delicate green cloth, upon which we place candles and small vases containing spring flowers, some of which the children have brought with them. Everywhere between them we place the coloured eggs. In the middle of the table is the large, round Easter loaf. The children help lay each place mat and plates and cups. Upon each plate we place one green or red serviette, and one of the small Easter loaves.

All these preparations take place roughly in the second half of the free-play period.

As on every festive day, after going to the toilet, washing and receiving a droplet of aromatic oil on their hands, the children sit on benches in the corridor. The adults take off their aprons. We start the festival with ring games based on the theme of seeking and finding. Then we sit down at the festive table where the candles are now lit, and say grace together. After this, the big Easter loaf is cut and shared out. At the end we wrap the little Easter loaves up in the paper serviettes for taking home. Once the candles have been extinguished, we go out into the garden to play in the sand pit or with skipping ropes and balls. But suddenly – what a surprise – one of the children comes running and shows a little Easter egg he's found. And now of course they all start hunting happily. We help the youngest ones a little because the eggs are so well hidden that no one noticed them earlier in the morning. From time to time a little verse is spoken as we hunt:

Under the beech

we're going to seek,
under the lime
we're going to find
a nest of hay
an egg of gold;
as the Easter hare
hops off, off, off and away.

Then we fetch a basket into which we put all the eggs that have been found, so we can share them out equally afterwards. One we eat straight away, and another we take home. These Easter eggs are homemade with rusk flour, grated hazelnuts, honey etc.[23]

The day ends with a fairy tale or Easter hare story, which brings us all together again to listen. On subsequent days the theme of seeking and finding echoes on in our rhythmic and ring games.

## *Between Easter and Whitsun*

There is a forty-day interval between Ash Wednesday and Palm Sunday; and after Easter comes another period of forty days up to Ascension Day. Now, unlike the two intersecting periods of Advent and Christmas, the two forty-day periods are separated from each other by the special time of Easter week.

There is an Easter mood in much of what the children now do outside, such as sowing and planting flowers and herbs in the garden, which children gladly take part in. There is special pleasure in sowing radishes since these can soon be harvested. If you don't have a garden, you can still grow things in pots on the windowsill or a veranda. Then there are the walks – so much to discover now! After a rainy day the path may be full of earthworms, which we carefully avoid stepping on. Or snails are placed beside each other in a row, to have a snail race. It doesn't matter if they don't all head in the same direction!

In the sand pit, the children are now busily digging and

building. Balls are flying through the air again, and skipping ropes are swinging back and forth. One can sense that the children's souls are absorbed and stimulated by this great power of resurrection and unfolding in nature. And now and again come moments of sudden stillness and wonder, when they observe, for instance, how a butterfly lands on a flower, or the birds twitter surprisingly loudly in the trees. There's a burgeoning wealth of flowers, as if earth were decorating itself for the loveliest celebration, and the sky with its deepening blue seems to come ever closer. In this mood the children reach for dandelion clocks to blow, as if they wanted to send heaven a greeting. In many kindergartens, with the same in mind, the children are allowed to blow coloured soap bubbles into the air.

# Whitsun

## *Preparing for Whitsun*

As Whitsun approaches we may ask how to give children some experience of the meaning of this festival, which child consciousness does not yet easily grasp. After Ascension, Christ's disciples felt bereft. But when they gathered on Whitsunday, they experienced the descent of the Holy Spirit upon them. From ancient times, all mythologies or works of art have depicted the reality of the spirit in images of white birds, swans, doves and storks. These were always seen to create a connection between the spiritual and earthly realms. The image of the stork indicates the soul approaching earth from the cosmos to unite with a body when a child is about to be born. The dove descending at the Jordan baptism is a particularly striking image, but we also find it in many Whitsun images and paintings of the annunciation.

Giving children a small, white Whitsun bird made of unspun sheep's wool is therefore a meaningful custom at this festival. Many days beforehand, we sing songs and play ring games involving birds, and the children pick this up in their free play and outdoors. Over several days the children see the kindergarten teacher making one little bird after another, and placing it in the large birds' nest (a shallow basket). Some children like helping with this, and make their own feathery creations, which then immediately find their way into their play. On some days, the whole free-play period is full of singing and playing with birds. There are also always children who blow little bits of wool or feathers into the air with delight. On the day before Whitsun we hang each bird on a green branch and place all of these together in a large vase, ready for the Whitsun festival.

*Making Whitsun birds*

Divide a skein of unspun, carded wool, about 35–40 cm (14–16 in) long, into three or four pieces, each of which will make one bird. Fold each in half and tie a knot to form the body. Push the knot so that the loop peeks out as a little head. Tease out the ends to make tail feathers. To form wings, attach a little teased wool under or over the body with a few stitches and shape the ends into points. You can also sew on two or three little curved feathers on each side. Feed the end of the sewing thread through the knot and out above the bird's back; this can later be used for hanging it up. The beak can either be carefully pulled out from the head and shaped, or you can take a tiny strand of red wool, twist it between thumb and forefinger and sew it on.

## Celebrating Whitsun in kindergarten

We celebrate our little Whitsun festival with the children on the last kindergarten day before Whitsun. We arrange the chairs in a circle, in the middle of which stands a stool, with three or four smaller footstools around it. A white cloth is spread over all the stools, and touches the ground between the small stools. On the large stool stands the vase with the hanging birds. Around it are candles and small vases of flowers, surrounded by white blossoming branches.

When the children come in from the garden, and as always before a festival are clean and tidy, we go into the room where the candles are already lit, and sit down in the circle. Accompanied by hand gestures we start saying some little bird verses and songs, such as:

The little bird builds a little nest
In a bush, where eggs may rest.
And out of these before too long

slip nestling birds, and sing their song.
O little bird, be cradled warm:
you can't fly yet. Keep safe and calm,
as you are rocked upon the branch –
I know you like this very much.
And when you've grown, then sing 'goodbye'
and fly off joyfully to the sky.

*H. Diestel*


Dear little bird, O flap your wings
bring sunshine to each child and sing,
dear bird, as summer grows from spring.

*A. Künstler*


To accompany this last verse the kindergarten teacher takes
one branch after another out of the vase and lets each bird fly to
a child. Instead of 'each child' she sings the child's actual name.
The song is sung as many times as there are children in the group.
Once they all have their bird, we let the birds fly about gently and
rhythmically to a verse such as this:

My pigeon house, I open wide
And I set all my pigeons free
They fly around on every side
And perch on the highest tree.
When they return from their merry flight,
They close their eyes and say 'Good night.'
Coo-oo Coo, Coo-oo Coo...


After this gesture of coming to repose, we finish with our daily
ending verse. Today, the little birds can be held in the children's
folded hands.

From my head to my feet
I am the image of God,
from my heart to my hands
I feel God's breath,
speaking with my mouth
I follow God's will.
When I see God
everywhere, in mother, father,
in all loving people,
in creatures, stones,
no fear is mine,
just love for all
that is around me.[24]

*Rudolf Steiner*

Singing quietly, we go out into the hallway where a few parents are already waiting to collect their children. The children take their birds home with them.

A few days later, the children will experience Whitsun at home. Clean, festive clothes, decorations of flowers, leafy birch twigs and candles give children a sense that this is an important festival for grown-ups. To begin with, children just connect words such as Ascension and Whitsun with festive days, and as they grow this connection is reinforced – providing an important foundation for their mature relationship with these festivals, when they can consider their underlying meaning.

# Summer

# St John's and Summertime

## *Creating the mood ourselves*

When midsummer arrives, and the sun reaches its highest point at the solstice; when the earth has breathed out completely and its soul, as though growing beyond itself, gives itself up to the cosmos; then we all, likewise, feel drawn out into the warmth and sunlight. We can enjoy the flourishing of nature with all our senses, and seek to grasp how heavenly forces reveal themselves in the natural world.

In ancient, pre-Christian mysteries, people used to gather from far and wide at midsummer and take part in long, rhythmic dances. Through these dances, they were lifted out of themselves, experiencing instead the revelations of the heavenly realms. As Emil Bock writes, 'The midsummer solstice was the moment when humans could receive the gifts of the gods.'[25]

This is no longer a useful path for us today: as free and aware beings, nowadays we need to seek *conscious* connection with the world of spirit.

John the Baptist stands at the turning point of transition between an older era and modern times. He came to prepare the way for the son of God who was willing to unite with the destiny of earthly humanity. And when John says, 'He must increase but I must decrease' (John 3:30), he is indicating this turning point. He recognised that the ancient wisdom mysteries must recede and human beings be released from guidance to seek the path to the divine, to Christ, in freedom. Paul was the first who was able to say, 'Not I, but Christ in me.'

These and other profound thoughts that we find in anthroposophy can engender in us the mood of St John's, which we need for our work with children.[26] The summer verses in Rudolf Steiner's *Calendar of the Soul* [27] can also be very helpful, or a verse such as the following:

> Sunlight streams through
> far breadths of space,
> birdsong rings out
> through open fields of air,
> the gift and grace of plants sprout from
> the being of earth;
> and, in gratitude, human souls
> lift themselves to the spirits of the world.

*Rudolf Steiner* [28]

A fairy tale such as the brothers Grimm's *Faithful John* also helps adults to get into the right mood for this season.

## St John's and summer with children

Young children experience the joys of summer through all their senses: dancing and singing, being outdoors in light, air and warmth, playing with water and sand. In the summer their play, however busy and happy, can also have a peaceful quality, a sense that they just want to dwell in the moment. It is as if they sense the turning point in the year, for at every reversal of a rhythm there is always a brief, scarcely noticeable pause. To be able to experience this inheld moment of high summer, children shouldn't stay out too long in fierce sunshine. They should all wear a sunhat and suncream, and we also ensure there are enough shady places under trees, bushes or parasols.

Children closely perceive the busy life of insects, for the summer air is full of them. Often a ladybird comes flying by, or a butterfly flutters about, or a honeybee or bumblebee drones past. At such moments we might say a few lines from the following poem, 'Our Lady's Little Glass'[29]:

Now flowers Our Lady's Little Glass:
wine in its clear chalice shines –
and here already come the guests
to the feast day of St John's.
Butterfly alights and sips
from the dainty flower's lips.
Honeybees dive in, and Bumble
in the goblet cheerfully rumbles.
Little midges gleefully dance
and beetles also get a chance
at St John's to taste the sweet
honey of heavenly delight.

*M. Garff*[30]

Our rhythmic games also include 'Shepherd Sevenshoes' who
wanders through forests and meadows with his sheep, and sees
the elves and glow-worms there.[31]

Here is another example of the many poems and songs for
children which express the summery mood:

**Sunflowers**

Sunflowers in the summer growing,
Growing up towards the light;
Light and warmth which draws them upwards,
Upwards striving in their might.

Mighty golden heads with seeds there,
Seeds to sleep in winter's ground;
Heads which turn from dawn till sunset
Following the sun's path round.

*Heather Thomas* [32]

In some kindergartens, the story of Lusmore with the hump who
meets the singing, dancing elves, is often told at this time of year.[33]

## St John's Day in kindergarten

June 24 is the birthday of St John the Baptist. The children can relate to him particularly as the closest friend of Jesus as a child, a connection which is beautifully expressed in the painting by Bernadino Luini, entitled "The Madonna and Child with Saint John', and also in various pictures by Raphael – for instance the 'Madonna of the Meadow'. One of these pictures will therefore be suitable for the seasonal nature table, upon which a yellow cloth now lies. The vases can be filled with roses, which blossom so plentifully at this season. And the children will often bring bunches of summer and meadow flowers to school, and perhaps sometimes an empty bird's nest.

For today's celebrations, we make a special St John's dish out of berries and honey, and eat this at beautifully laid tables decorated with roses. During free play, the kindergarten teacher makes very delicate butterflies from coloured, unspun sheep's wool (magic wool). We hang these up on the flowers by thin threads, or place them on the nature table (see p. 11). Naturally, some of the children will come to join in, and will produce lovely butterflies by imitation. Occasionally a child will fix a bit of wool to a thread and call it a bee, bumblebee or fly, depending on the colour, and then make it fly around, perhaps with an accompanying song or little verse.

The St John's fire we light today is a special event. We set it alight in the garden after our morning snack (taking all due safety precautions). In preparation for this, in the preceding days we have chopped up branches and fetched old things from the cellar that have been kept for this purpose. Expectantly the children stand around and watch as the fire is built. What excitement when the flames leap up, sparks fly and there's a crackling and blazing! They watch with delight as an old brush, worn-out fir cones, or perhaps a broken broom or an old basket, are devoured by the flames, making space for something new.

It is important that the children do not start to play around the fire, but keep a necessary respect for it. The kindergarten teacher will give an example of this. Carefully and attentively she receives the pieces of wood and objects which the children pass her and places them in the fire. Now and again a child will step back from the increasing heat. And once everything has been burned, the flames gradually diminish and soon only the red-hot glow can be seen at the centre, along with the strong pungency of the fire.

Depending on circumstances, we cither tell a story close up to the waning fire or go inside to the story corner.[34]

*Butterflies from coloured wool*

You will need: pipe-cleaners; unspun, coloured sheep's wool (magic wool); various colours of sewing thread. Follow the diagrams overleaf.

Wrap a 3 cm (1 1/4 in) piece of pipe-cleaner very finely in a little coloured wool. At the upper end, pull the wool out a little beyond the pipe-cleaner, divide it into two and twist each strand between finger and thumb. This makes the butterfly's feelers. Now take a little very finely teased wool of the same colour and shape the two upper wings from it; then, with a further piece of wool, the two lower wings. Now place the two pairs of wings together and decorate them, for instance by placing a round spot in a darker tone or different colour on each wing, surrounded by a brighter or darker colour tone. Finally, place the body (pipe-cleaner) in the middle (a), fold the wings upwards together (b) and, using a corresponding thread colour, sew the body on from below. Push the needle diagonally upwards through the body and draw the thread out, so that the butterfly can be hung from it (c).

It's worth emphasising that only a little wool is needed, and the more finely it's teased out, the better the different layers will combine. If the layers of wool don't bind well enough, hold an iron above the butterfly with hot steam coming out – but don't actually iron!

If you don't have any pipe-cleaners to hand, you can make the butterfly as follows: make a knot in a strand of wool measuring roughly 10–12 cm (4–5 in). This will later be the end of the body (1). Then make two further knots above each other with the two ends (2) to form the head. Tease out the ends to form the butterfly feelers, twist them between finger and thumb to form points, and then shorten as needed. Finely tease the wool for the wings, pass through the body, and then decorate as above. The thread for hanging up the butterfly, which is fed through the two body strands, will hold the wing wool together adequately (3).

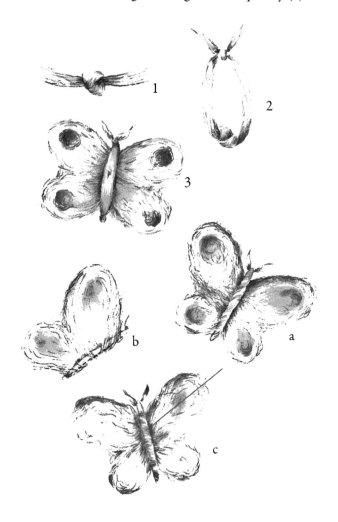

# Summer Festival

We can regard the summer festival we celebrate in the larger community of parents and siblings, outside in the garden, as the culmination of everything we have already said about the time of St John's. Before we look in more detail at this festival, which centres around games and playing, we will describe the various preparations which children can share in.

## Preparing for the summer festival

### Flower crowns

Each child should have a flower crown to wear at the festival. We braid plaits of raffia or velvet, making them the right size for each child's head, and give each a nametag. The children then take these home, and there, on the morning of the festival, flowers are put into the plait. These crowns can then be used again each year, after readjustments.

### Coloured bunting

We make coloured strings of bunting to demarcate different game areas in the garden. We stretch a long string, not too thin, between two stands, and attach colour-balanced crêpe-paper strips to it. The strips, roughly 50 cm (20 in) long and 3 cm (1 in) wide, are folded in half, the loop is placed over the string, the ends pushed through the loop and carefully drawn tight. Several children at a time can stand by the string and help, since the attached strips can easily be pushed back and forwards.

*Games and gifts*

Various games can take place during the festival, which can incorporate little gifts for the children. For the game 'Little bell in the ring', we choose a little bell or 'flutterball' as a small gift. Flutterballs are a wonderful symbol of the summer and the summer's turning point when they fly high in the air, turn round suddenly and, in their headlong descent, flutter their coloured ribbons. Flutterballs are made of a round piece of bright fabric (25–30 cm, 10–12 in diameter) filled with very fine woodshavings or sawdust and a small stone in the middle. Before tying the balls up, place the ends of yellow, orange and red crêpe-paper strips, about 50 cm (20 in) long and 2–3 cm (1 in) wide, inside as streamers.

We play the fishing lake game, for which we make little fruit-jelly fishes, which the children can catch (see p. 64). We build an obstacle path, in which the children can find little bark boats as gifts. We play a ship-pulling game in which little boats on strings are 'loaded' with a strawberry or other fruit.

*Arrangements in the garden*

The day before the festival we build the various play areas in the garden using boards, logs and stones: the fishing-lake surround, the harbour and sitting logs for the ship-pulling game, and the obstacle course. Usually there's a good deal of excitement in the air since there's much to be moved and carted about, and often the children already start having a go at parts of the obstacle course.

This shared activity means that the children already know what awaits them, and so don't get too overexcited on the actual day.

## Celebrating the summer festival

In our kindergarten this festival usually takes place on Saturday morning. A few children who come early help with the final preparations – for instance decorating the play areas with coloured bunting. The lake is given a blue cloth, and on this we place shells and the fruit-jelly fish (the small catching wire on each fish must point vertically upwards). The obstacle path is given a river, tunnel and slide. In various places we set up parasols and seats, for parents and grandparents to have a rest.

At ten o'clock all the other children arrive with their parents. Crowned in flowers and in a festive mood, we gather and process outside, singing, 'Tra-ri-ra, the summer is here...' and first form a big dancing circle together. Then the children, accompanied by their parents, set off for the various games, allowing the kindergarten teacher to move around freely and keep an eye on everything.

When the children and parents are all happily playing games, with flutterballs flying high in the air between parents and children, and the grandparents are sitting beside the water tubs, watching the ships sail over the water, we really have a lovely sense of midsummer.

After all the children have had a go at all the games, they gather on either side of the 'harbour' and watch their parents pulling ships. This is a special joy for the children because we see which ship sails fastest – which was of no consequence earlier when the children were playing the game.

Finally we gather together once more and all dance lively summer dances.

In some kindergartens the summer festival is celebrated in the afternoon and starts with a *Sleeping Beauty* ring game, after which there is coffee, juice and cakes at beautifully laid tables. Then the children go off to play all the games, followed by dancing. At the end, in some kindergartens, they each get a colourful tissue-paper butterfly attached to a little rod. Accompanied by a song, it flies to each child.

Elsewhere, the summer festival starts by carrying out the 'summer tree' – a wreath attached to a tall pole decorated with coloured ribbons. Everyone follows to where the summer dances then take place.

Sometimes, too, a puppet show marks the end of the celebrations, or a song sung together by everyone.

Of course there are all sorts of other possibilities. The important thing is not to let it go on too long, nor overtax the children. Then they will remain fairly calm to the end, and afterwards when they get back home.

# Farewell Festival (for children going to big school)

This little festival takes place in the summer, at the end of the school year. Together with parents, the whole kindergarten group says farewell to the children who are leaving to go into Class 1.

## Preparing for the farewell festival

### The schoolchild doll

Long before there is any talk of the farewell festival, the 'schoolchildren' can make their own, simple knotted dolls. This is done during the free-play period over the last five to six months. The younger children join in the happy atmosphere through imitation. Before the dolls are made, however, we embroider a soft cloth to wrap them in on an embroidery frame. This may be done during the winter. We do it properly, walking the needle across the cloth with beautiful, coloured threads (avoiding anything representational). Whether only a corner or the whole cloth is embroidered depends on the individual child. Children are never prevented from playing by the need to do this activity.

When at last the soft pink flannel cloths are ready for the dolls, the children want to make their own 'newborn baby', which they have been looking forward to for so long. The only help needed is in tying the neck thread and perhaps tying the knots for the hands. Each child draws on eyes and mouth with a crayon, and threads on hair. Whether the head has three hairs, a whole head full or none at all is again up to the individual child, as is its wardrobe. They can also sew not only clothes, jackets with buttons and little pockets but also bibs, swimming trunks and sunhats. The children only need help with cutting out fabric, to make sure the clothes really fit. They are never made to sew hems or pleats. They finish their stitches and where needed sew a running stitch for pulling tight around the neck. Children often like to make a cloth bed in which the doll can sleep, but it is important for them to have their doll to play with in their games – even if it's only lying in the furthest corner of the 'workshop' or on the 'back seat of the car'.

*Framed picture*

In the time after Easter, each schoolchild can choose an art postcard from a wide selection. To make a frame for this, the kindergarten teacher saws a symmetrical plywood board, 2.5–3 cm (1 in) larger than the card all round. The edges and surfaces of this are finely sanded, waxed and polished. All these activities, which take place over many days during free play, usually draw enthusiastic help from all the children, not just the schoolchildren. The white edges of each card are cut off, and it's glued to the board to the reverse of which a hook is attached. The children listen attentively to the name of the painter which, written on a special little label, is also glued to the back of the board. Finally, all the pictures are wrapped in fine tissue paper tied with a ribbon, and a nametag is attached. Then they are put away in the far corner of a cupboard until the farewell festival.

*Picture folders*

A few days before the farewell festival, we make cords from twisted woollen threads and use these to bind together each child's watercolour paintings (A3 size) and wax crayon drawings (A4) into a 'picture book'. These are pictures from the child's whole time in kindergarten. We choose an especially beautiful picture to go on the front cover.

*String puppet play*

We can also create the scene for the puppet play which we will present at the festival with the help of the schoolchildren. We usually present the fairy tale of Sleeping Beauty, since it offers plenty for everyone to do. The schoolchildren sit to the right and left of the kindergarten teacher and manipulate two-stringed puppets, which are relatively easy to handle. Children sitting in an outer semi-circle play freely on the children's harps at certain points in the play. Two or three days before the festival, we perform the play to the other children in the group.

*Preparing the room*

The final preparations are made on the morning of the festival. We put a small round table in the centre of the room, covered with a festive yellow cloth and as many candles as there are schoolchildren. In the middle of the table stands the big kindergarten candle. We decorate the table with flowers from the garden.

A stool stands ready around the table, covered in a cloth, for each departing schoolchild, and on this we place the picture books, the gift (framed picture) and the lovingly made doll. Over this we spread a yellow cloth, on top of which we place a crown made of gold cardboard.

Finally we set up a circle of chairs around this, and then the festival can begin.

## Celebrating the festival with parents

We celebrate the festival during the last hour of the morning (on the last day of term) or sometimes the afternoon before. The schoolchildren are fully aware of their 'dignity' and make their best efforts. This is particularly apparent in the puppet play with which the festival begins. The children are fully immersed in their individual tasks and listen carefully to the teacher's narration. After the play we sit down in a large circle in such a way that the schoolchildren each sit in front of their own little table. The parents sit beside their child and the other children sit in between. First the schoolchildren light their small candles from the big candle then remain standing in front of their crown stools. The kindergarten teacher now goes from one to the other and places the crowns on their heads. At this moment it often seems as if the children grow beyond themselves towards their crowns. Then we sing and mime playing on our 'flutes' and 'violins'. After this I tell a little story that I have made up especially for these children.

After this we talk about the events in the past weeks that have shown which children are the 'schoolchildren'. For instance, how the teacher has had to become a dentist on occasion, and help pull wobbly teeth; or how a schoolchild took over mixing the cake dough on one occasion when the teacher was busy; or how the teacher heard a child asking for a needle to be threaded and another said, 'Shall I do it for you?' The children nod their heads happily when they hear these little anecdotes. Then we look ahead a little to what awaits the children when they go to big school – for instance, one day a teacher will come into the classroom and say, *'Bonjour, mes chers enfants,'* because they will learn to speak as people speak in France.

It's now also time to unveil the gifts on the stool. With accustomed care, the children will fold up the cloth and then first open their framed picture. In doing so some children experience a kind of joy of rediscovery, calling out, 'Yes, that's the picture I chose!' Now they slowly walk around the group to show all the parents and children their pictures.

While the children wrap up their own pictures, we share out pieces of fruit amongst all the children and parents. Finally the schoolchildren take their dolls in their arms and we rock them, with all children and parents accompanying this with singing, and cradling gestures. We end the festival with our usual daily verse, pointing out that in Class 1 the schoolchildren will have a new verse to say. Then each extinguishes their candle with the snuffer.

Of course there are many other ways of organising the farewell festival. In some groups, for instance, the little festival first takes place in a circle, followed by the puppet play to end with. Or there may be a special story instead of the puppet play. In some kindergartens, the festival is celebrated without the younger children present, just with the schoolchildren and their parents.

In our kindergarten a teacher would sometimes be leaving at the same time, and then of course all the parents and children, and the new teacher, were present. And at the end of the festival we all witnessed the departing teacher passing the kindergarten key in a ceremonial manner to the colleague who was replacing her.

# Autumn

# Harvest Time

## *Creating the mood ourselves*

Once the sun has reached its highest point at St John's, ripening and fruiting begin to come into their own. We gratefully receive the first gifts of nature, which follow in abundance through the autumn. However, we don't only offer thanks for what we receive but also for everything that has contributed to the growth and flourishing. Our thanks are directed also to the life of the soil, the light and warmth of the sun, the wind and life-giving rain, the animal world in all its diversity, and the energy and activity of human beings. Thus gratitude can accompany us throughout the year and, when we think about it, is really owed to all realms of life. This is one of the most important virtues to nurture in children during the first seven years, but solely through imitation. This deep-rooted gratitude, kindled in the kindergarten, transforms in the schoolchild into the capacity for love; and later, in the adolescent, is enhanced and extended into love of action and a sense of duty.[35]

In autumn we connect gratitude with the harvest festival, which celebrates the moment when all the corn for our daily bread has ripened and been harvested.

We decorate the seasonal nature table with a golden-yellow cloth, with fruits from the garden, woods and fields, and bright autumn flowers. If you wish to add an art image, suitable pictures can be found by Van Gogh, who painted typical harvest scenes and gestures, or by Millet – to name two examples.

## Activities with children

After the summer holidays, when the new school year begins, autumn is fast approaching and the first harvesting starts. Fruits from our gardens or those brought by children can be made into preserves and jellies or dried, accompanied by delicious aromas.[30] With wonder we find a star in every apple that we slice open crossways. And unconsciously children experience how heaven with its stars works itself into the form of fruits. While cutting up apples, we meet a little worm from time to time. Yes indeed, that little fellow knew which the tastiest apples were – and so we leave him a little piece of apple and put him with it on the compost heap. There's no question of disgust, and children sense without any instruction that everything in the world has its rightful place. The carrots and radishes which we pull out of the vegetable patch in the garden taste especially good. And the slices of carrot, compared with the apple, reveal more of a solar quality – for in every slice we can find a little sun. We smell lovely aromas while gathering leaves of lemon balm, thyme and sage, which we will later make into tea or use when cooking.

The time of gathering and harvesting has begun, and so we take little baskets with us when we go on walks, to collect rosehips, beechnuts, conkers, acorns and colourful leaves. We also spend a lot of time with the different sheaves of grain, from which we can weave a large harvest wreath. For days the children sit amidst a mountain of straw, helping to cut the stems to length or making themselves straws for playing with. Most of the straw is bundled up again and kept for late autumn when the rose bushes must be protected for the winter, or for making a new roof for the birdtable. We will also need a little for the crib in Advent. The remaining straw is burned in the small fireplace outside, to the children's excitement.

Now we start threshing the ears of wheat, an activity which continues for several days. To do this we lay a large cloth on the floor, and around it thick, folded cloths as knee cushions. In the middle stands a basket with ears of corn, another for the threshed ears, and a bowl for the grain. Children each have a small branch with which they hammer on an ear until all the grains have come out. They can be heard saying the verse which they know from a ring game: 'We're threshing, we're threshing, we're threshing the corn...' After this, they collect their grain in their little wooden bowls. Of course many grains and husks remain behind on the cloth. These will later be carefully poured into a large wooden bowl. Next the teacher lifts some grain up in their hand and, as they let them pour back slowly into the bowl, we blow the husks away on the wind. We don't want to lose a single grain.

Next the grain is milled with a hand-mill. Even the three-year-olds want to be the miller for a moment or two. Apart from a hand-mill one can also give the children old coffee grinders for milling, with the screws set not too tight. Milling like this is hard work, and the grinders must be held firmly between the knees. For some of the bigger children, this is a welcome challenge. The resulting coarse meal then has to be milled a second time, which is easier.

We use the meal to bake the big harvest loaf. While one group may, as a blessing, engrave the sign of the cross on the round loaf, another group may draw sunrays on it. On the day before the festival we decorate the corn wreath with nuts and fruits.

## The harvest festival

We invite parents to attend our harvest festival. For parents new to the kindergarten this is a wonderful opportunity to become better acquainted with kindergarten life and the parent community. On the morning of the festival, the children bring baskets that they have carefully arranged with a grown-up at home, containing washed fruit, vegetables and flowers from the garden; or, if they don't have a garden, things they have found on a walk. Mostly these little baskets are beautifully decorated with flowers and colourful leaves. All the baskets are placed on the harvest table in the middle of the room. The great round loaf occupies the centre of the table, surrounded by flowers, ears of corn and candles.

We begin the festival altogether, parents and children, with the harvest ring game, which we have been playing almost every day in preceding weeks. After this we sit down in a big circle around the harvest table and light the candles. We say the grace by Christian Morgenstern, which we all know well, and which encompasses the whole of Creation in simple words:

Earth who gave to us this food,
sun who made it ripe and good:
dear earth, dear sun by you we live,
our loving thanks to you we give.

Then everyone forms a little receiving bowl with their hands and is given a piece of bread. As we share this out we sing a song about where the bread has come from. Without prompting, everyone waits until the last person has received their bread and the song has fallen quiet. Honey-salt bread has to be chewed really well, so we sit quietly together and enjoy the taste. Afterwards the children offer the teacher a little fruit from their basket (apples, pears or plums). With the help of two adults, we cut this into pieces, place them on plates, and the children pass these to everyone in the big circle. We end the meal as we do every day, by holding hands and saying:

For food and drinks
we give our thanks.

After the candles have been extinguished, everyone goes outside into the garden, where the parents light a little fire and wrap potatoes, which have been partially pre-cooked, in silver foil. While the potatoes are cooking in the fire, the children watch the flames or play in the sand or in the meadow, or help arrange wooden stumps around the fire for sitting on. Then at last the first potatoes are taken out of the fire with long tongs or sticks, the foil is removed and they are eaten. To end the festival, each child receives a little bunch of corn with a strawflower, which was made in the preceding days from different types of corn, in the presence and with the help of the children.

Looking back we can say that this festival is a culmination of a long harvesting period. Our thanks – this time for once actually expressed in words – lives in an unconscious and less articulated form in every gesture through the weeks of preparation. For many days after the harvest festival we continue to have a special morning snack with the fruit and nuts from the children's baskets. Again, there will be plenty of opportunities for the children to help. Especially popular, for instance, are 'potato men',[37] accompanied by grated carrots and apple, honey-salt bread with butter and herbs, or a vegetable soup.

And so the festival echoes on a little, in a lovely fashion. The harvest wreath, which now hangs without fruits under the overhanging roof outside, is visited by a flock of sparrows who each day leave behind a scattering of husks and chaff.

# Michaelmas

## *Creating the mood ourselves*

Having considered the great gathering of fruits at harvest time, let's now look at a further aspect of this season. In tracing the earth's great in-breath, which starts after the summer solstice and continues through to the winter solstice, we find ourselves standing at a clear threshold at Michaelmas, at the end of September. It's as if light and darkness here face and challenge each other. The days become noticeably shorter – in other words, external sunlight diminishes, and life forces wane from natural processes. But as human beings we can set something against this dying away of nature by trying to take up summer sunlight into ourselves, and preserving it within us. Then, towards the period of deepest winter, it can transform inwardly into the soul light which illumines Christmas. This will happen all the more if we can cross the autumn threshold to Michaelmas in full consciousness.

As days grow short
hearts grow bright.
Saint Michael with his sword
shines out against the night.

Saint Michael, lord
of our times: to us
you give true bread.
You clothe us in new dress!

*Heinz Ritter*

Before we consider how to celebrate Michaelmas with children, let's ask how we as adults can find some relationship to this festival, which has no past tradition to draw on.

In Chapter 12 of the Book of Revelation, mighty images are conveyed of the battle of the archangel Michael with the dragon: 'And there was war in heaven: Michael and his angels fought against the dragon; and the dragon fought and his angels...' Michael succeeds in vanquishing the dragon, and hurls him to the earth. 'Woe to the inhabiters of the earth and of the sea! For the devil is come down unto you...' (Revelation 12:12).

We can sense the deep relevance of this image to contemporary humanity if we look back to earlier epochs. According to the accounts of Paradise in the Bible, at an early stage of evolution we were still intimately connected with the divine world, and lived close to God. After being banished from Eden, we focused our attention ever more strongly on the world of the senses, discovering the material world's attributes, and schooling our rational capacities in relation to it. As a consequence, our connection with the divine, spiritual world increasingly faded, and we felt ourselves ever more free and independent. On the earth, however, lives the expelled power of evil, of darkness or – to remain with the images of the Apocalypse – the dragon. He seeks to distract and divert us from the spiritual realm, and to chain us to the material world. Daily we can witness his rampages in violence, destruction, hatred, lies and much more, and can have a clear sense that great exertion, strength and alertness are required to oppose these forces. But in these inner and outward efforts, we can count on the help of spiritual beings if we do not close ourselves off from them. Here Michael acquires special importance.

The dragon from heaven is hurled by Michael
if you can vanquish your own inner turmoil.

*Angelus Silesius*

Since the dawn of time there have been so-called mystery or initiation centres on earth, where those who were called to do so underwent intensive spiritual schooling. There they developed the capacity to consciously cultivate a relationship with the world of spirit, and to have spiritual vision. These were the high priests or initiates who accompanied humanity on its evolutionary path through long eras, leading it increasingly towards autonomy and freedom. Today we stand entirely on our own two feet, and can seek a connection with higher worlds through our own powers of consciousness, and solely out of inner freedom.

The archangel Michael is regarded as a special protector of such mystery and initiation centres. And so we can say that his concern is to once more redirect our capacity for knowledge – which has become increasingly entangled in matter – towards perception of spiritual realities. As such, he stands more than ever in a battle with the powers of darkness. The arena of this battle is both around us and in us. Each day we can experience these battles within ourselves: for instance, in trying to overcome our own inner lethargy. If we succeed in gaining the upper hand over forces that seek to distract us, we can feel connected with the Michael powers that accompany us on a courageous and energetic path of development.

In the most diverse regions of the earth we find churches, chapels and mountains dedicated to the archangel Michael. Many such places indicate that in earlier times they were the site of mystery centres or Michael revelations. The extent to which Michael has long been revered can be seen, for example, from the following Celtic hymn, from the *Carmina Gadelica* by Alexander Carmichael:[38]

### Michael, the Victorious

Thou Michael the victorious,
I make my circuit under thy shield,
Thou Michael of the white steed,
And of the bright brilliant blades,
Conqueror of the dragon,

Be thou at my back,
Thou ranger of the heavens,
Thou warrior of the King of all,
O Michael the victorious,
My pride and my guide,
O Michael the victorious,
The glory of mine eye.

I make my circuit
In the fellowship of my saint,
On the machair, on the meadow,
On the cold heathery hill;
Though I should travel ocean
And the hard globe of the world
No harm can ever befall me
'Neath the shelter of thy shield;
O Michael the victorious,
Jewel of my heart,
O Michael the victorious,
God's shepherd thou art.

Be the sacred Three of Glory
Aye at peace with me,
With my horses, with my cattle,
With my woolly sheep in flocks.
With the crops growing in the field
Or ripening in the sheaf,
On the machair, on the moor,
In cole, in heap, or stack.
Every thing on high or low,
Every furnishing and flock,
Belong to the holy Triune of glory,
And to Michael the victorious.

In old pictures we find representations of Michael fighting
the dragon, where he bears either a lance or a sword. We also see

images of Michael with a pair of scales or a cosmic globe. If we contemplate such pictures they can help us form a more conscious connection with the being of Michael.

The lance is an image of clear focus upon a goal, but at the same time has a quality of self-distancing, since it lets one fight at a distance from one's adversary. We do the same thing with our awareness when we initially focus on a situation, and through thinking, seek objective distance from it. Michael's lance hits its target but his gaze is not directed towards it, suggesting that his inner strength is capable of vanquishing his opponent.

The sword, on the other hand, is an image of sundering: in other words, once we have focused clearly on something, it's possible for our thinking to separate one aspect from another. We also speak of sharp or honed thinking. In many works of art we see Michael raising the sword above his head, as if it were gaining impetus from the sphere of thoughts.

We find a further attribute in the image of the scales. What we have first focused clearly on and divided in thought must then be weighed up – by making a moral decision. The process of weighing leads us to a resting centre where balance is achieved. In us, too, once clarity has been gained, the heart needs to speak. Thus the image of Michael with the scales embodies the interplay of our wakeful intelligence with our emotions.

The globe is an image of the all-encompassing unity of the cosmos and earth, of the universe. Michael with the globe shows us he is connected with all cosmic events in the heavens and on earth.

These initial thoughts about the figure of Michael must also include the soul quality of courage, which Michael embodies. He does not give way but courageously takes up his task and draws on inner soul strength in overcoming his adversary.

Young children can experience qualities of courage in fairy tales, when they hear how a king's son meets tasks and trials, and manages to overcome setbacks. They identify with such a figure – feel fear and joy as they listen; and this strengthens their capacity for courage. They also learn from adults that one can overcome fear, which is why they trustingly seek protection from us. 'Tests of courage' or 'trials of endurance', in the sense of outward challenges, are not appropriate until children reach school age (6+) at the earliest.

## *The Michaelmas festival*

We celebrate Michaelmas Day on September 29 in the small group without parents.

Today a red cover lies on the seasonal nature table, which is decorated with colourful autumn leaves, foliage and perhaps sunflowers. In the middle stands the picture of Michael, possibly an icon such as Michael bearing the globe. Paintings on a gold background are particularly suitable for younger children, as gold indicates cosmic wisdom – with which they still have an instinctive relationship.

When the first children arrive in the morning, we prepare the dough for the festive cake, which the children cover all over, and very carefully, with thin apple slices. In some kindergartens, loaves or rolls are baked. Soon the rooms are filled with delicious aromas, and we all look forward to our morning snack. But first we polish the lovely red apples that are placed in a shallow basket, in the middle of which stands a candleholder with a big candle. Now and then one of the younger children may come to me and ask, 'What are you doing?' And on hearing the reply, 'Today is Michaelmas Day', she runs off again happily to tell the others – 'Today is Michaelmas Day!'

Next we push the tables together to form a long table, as we sometimes do on festive days. It's usually the five- and six-year-olds who immediately gather to lay and decorate the festive table. One lays the tablemats, another the plates and spoons. On each plate we place a red or yellow paper serviette folded into a triangle, and on top of this a golden ribbon. Along the middle of the long table we put a red, narrowly-folded cloth, and on this come vases of flowers and candles. By now almost all the children have left their play and gathered round the table. With big, expectant eyes they watch everything that's happening.

Once the room is ready, we place a little table in the middle, and on it the basket with polished apples and the candle. Now it's time to go to the washroom, where the children have their hair combed for the festive occasion, and each receive a tiny drop of aromatic oil to rub on their hands. In the hallway the adults take off their aprons, and then we process around the lit candle making the Michael gesture,[39] bearing the little sword of Michael, and singing a suitable Michael song. Then we say the following Michael verse, which we also accompany with a gesture:

When we come to the golden door
Michael stands there before:
With his great sword of light he girds
the earth in the blessing of his words.

*E. Palmer-Paulsen*

After repeating both song and verse twice, the kindergarten teacher gives one child after another an apple from the basket, placing it in hands formed like a little bowl. We carry this apple to the festive table and place it on the serviette on the plate. After lighting the candles for our festive meal, the children, one after another, give their apple to an adult who cuts it crossways to reveal the star in the middle. The children are always amazed anew when they open up their apple themselves and find the star, hidden in the darkness of the apple, revealed like a wonder. Around the star some children will often discover little 'spraying star sparks'. After this, the children wrap their apples in the serviettes, tying them with the gold ribbon to take home with them.

We have chosen to make the apple a central part of our Michaelmas festival because it is the archetypal fruit, and also the fruit of the tree of knowledge. Michael has a special connection with our cognitive faculties and powers of knowledge, as mentioned earlier (see p. 118).

After the festive meal, depending on the weather, we either go out into the garden or go for a walk. If the wind is blowing well, we may take a few sheets of paper (just very simply folded) and string, and let little 'dragons' flutter behind us.

We end the day with a suitable fairy tale, which is repeated on the following days.

During these Michaelmas days the children like making a 'proper sword'. They take two simple sticks that they tie together with a piece of string, and carry in a string tied around their tummy. To adults such a 'sword' – like the knotted doll – may not look like much, but in the child's imagination, especially after their own efforts at making it, it is 'real' and 'shining', and is carried around with great dignity.

Over the years we have made various changes to the way we celebrate Michaelmas in our kindergarten, and the present form may also only be tentative. For this festival in particular, for which no past traditions exist, we have to keep seeking appropriate forms.

In many kindergartens, Michaelmas and the harvest festival are celebrated together, as one festival, and this also has its deep significance. It all depends on our own perspective and preference, which we freely and creatively choose.

If these two autumn festivals are celebrated together, kindergarten life is filled with harvesting activities up to the day before the festival. On Michaelmas Day itself, as already described, the seasonal nature table is strikingly altered. The big, festive table is laid and decorated with special care, and a central place is given to the harvest loaf, surrounded by candles, ears of corn and flowers. Over the nature table a harvest wreath may hang, or the harvest crown, decorated with fruits.

The Michael ring game will take the place of the harvest ring game. Here children take it in turn to be dressed up in a red cloak and golden helmet and sword, to be St George, who embodies the spirit of the archangel Michael in human form.

If you celebrate the harvest and Michaelmas festivals separately, it's a good idea to ensure they do not follow each other too quickly. As far as the harvest festival is concerned, I don't feel tied to any particular date; I just make sure it's celebrated at least a week before Michaelmas, and that parents can be involved as described. It's also too much to have two, equally big autumn celebrations, and so we accentuate them differently. My preference is to have a large festival at the start of the school year, when parents and children can meet each other and participate actively in the new social community. For me, the start of Michaelmas has, in contrast, a more intimate character.

# Lantern Time

In late autumn, when the sun often scarcely penetrates the wind-blown clouds, and when the days grow ever shorter and darker, children go out into the twilight with their lanterns. It's as if they have received the last gift of sunlight and now, carefully protecting it, they carry it singing before them. It's not yet time to light the first candle indoors to mark the first day of Advent as the beginning of ever-increasing inner light towards Christmas.

At this time of year the seasonal nature table can be decorated with a gnome's cave made of roots and dry moss.

Two lantern festivals mark this time. From the Celtic tradition there is Halloween on October 31, and from Continental Europe we have Martinmas on November 11. Halloween is connected with the earth, and its turnip or pumpkin lanterns are made of fruits from the ground. Martinmas commemorates a human deed of sharing, and its paper lanterns are entirely made by human hand. As the outer light of day diminishes, there is first a kind of afterglow of light given by the earth – the turnip or pumpkin lanterns. Then there is the human spark of kindness we see in the paper lanterns of Martinmas. The light is gradually transformed from the outer light of the sun in summer to the internal spirit light of Advent and Christmas.

## Halloween [40]

Halloween is celebrated each year on October 31. This festival has its roots with the Celts of Great Britain, and was originally a celebration of their new year (Samhain): the end of the harvest season and the beginning of the season of darkness and cold. Sacred bonfires were lit and people wore costumes made of animal heads and skins. When the celebration was over, they re-lit their home hearth fires from the sacred bonfire to protect them during the coming winter. The Celts also believed that just before new year, the boundary between the worlds of the living and the dead became blurred.

Around the eighth century, the Christian church designated November 1 as All Saints' Day to honour saints and martyrs. The celebration was also called All Hallows and the night before it became known as All Hallows Eve and, eventually, Hallowe'en.

The tradition of dressing in costume for Halloween has both European and Celtic roots. Hundreds of years ago, people feared they would encounter ghosts if they left their homes on Halloween, when the boundaries between the worlds of the living and dead were thin. To avoid being recognised by the dead, people wore masks when they left their homes after dark. On Halloween, people would also put bowls of food outside their homes as an offering to the ghosts.

The American Halloween tradition of 'trick-or-treating' has roots in the early All Souls' Day parades in England, when poor families would beg for food, and more affluent families would give them special pastries called 'soul cakes' in return for promises to pray for the family's dead relatives. In the nineteenth century, Halloween began to lose all religious significance, becoming a secular children's holiday of trick-or-treating. Families could prevent tricks being played on them by providing the neighbourhood children with treats. Thus an American tradition arose and has continued to grow.

Now in the US, Halloween has become a huge industry – a commercialised experience with mass-produced costumes and an evening of collecting as much packaged candy as possible. The Halloween festival we celebrate in kindergarten with young children provides a creative and imaginative alternative for both children and parents.

*Preparing for Halloween*

Halloween is a festival of the night, so in many kindergartens the children don't wear costumes to school, but celebrate an evening Halloween festival with families instead.

A wonderful activity for the children during the day in kindergarten is carving pumpkin lanterns. And the faces they make on the pumpkins tell so much about each child. The pumpkins can be used for the evening festival, so the children get a chance to make something that will be shared with everyone.

As an extended preparation, kindergarten teachers can plant pumpkin seeds with children in the spring, and care for the developing plants until autumn when they can be harvested. (Make sure someone checks on the plants during the summer vacation.)

As preparation for the Halloween festival, the parents of each kindergarten group, in collaboration with their teacher, choose a short fairy tale or nursery rhyme (in the US, this is called a 'skit'). They decide who will act their little play and they provide a 'treat', such as a homemade nutritious snack, a small stone or a shell treasure (see p. 134 for suggestions of suitable gifts). All of this is done as a gift, and is kept secret from the children until they experience the magic of the evening for themselves.

Parents are given guidelines by the teachers on suitable costumes to make for their children, which support children's developing creative imaginations, and are not too gory, skimpy or suggestive, as many of the commercially available costumes are.

*Celebrating Halloween*

In the early evening on Halloween, as soon as it grows dark, the festival begins. Grown-ups in costumes perform their skits, and each of the five or six groups gives the children a little treat. The pathway from skit to skit is lit by paper lanterns and the jack-o-lanterns (pumpkin lanterns) which the children carved in kindergarten.

The costumed children and their parents are led along the magical pathway from 'station' to 'station' by adults dressed as 'angel guides'. There is little talking as the angel guides lead the way, quietly singing, carrying lanterns of their own.

This is a creative and imaginative festival for all, and can even offer an early bedtime for children. The adults' own creativity is stimulated and given a chance for expression.

## Martinmas

### Preparing with children

After Michaelmas, there are all sorts of things to be done outside in the garden before winter arrives. We clear the flowerbeds, dig them over and replant flower bulbs removed in early summer. Some shrubs and perennial herbs need cutting back. By the time the beds are covered in brushwood, the wind will have already blown many leaves from the trees and we can rake them up well into November, and carry them to the compost heap in large baskets. At the same time the children busily collect big and small pebbles and use these to build little gnome houses in tree roots or secret corners, often with beautiful front gardens. It's already very cold on some days, and sunlight has waned noticeably. On the day of the lantern festival we place tea-lights in the gnome's houses, so that the gnomes can also have a little candlelight during the festival.

Throughout this period we have been working on our lanterns each day during the free-play period. These are very simply made from sheets of paper, painted with watercolours, which are then oiled and glued around round Camembert cheese boxes; these provide structures for the base and upper rim.[41] The edges of the cheese boxes can easily be cut in a decorative wave pattern if you like. Sticking gold foil on the edges is not really appropriate yet, since the first touch of gold belongs in Advent. Until the festival, the lanterns are hung up across a corner of the room on a string.

## The lantern festival

On the late afternoon of lantern festival day, all the children and parents gather for a puppet play, whose scenery the children have busily helped set up in preceding days. Outside it's already getting dark. After fortifying ourselves with apple cake, we go out with the lit lanterns. The children are astonished when they see all the little lights burning in all the gnome houses! The children go from one house to another, shining their lanterns into dark corners to see if they can see a hedgehog, a little mouse or maybe even a gnome. Then we go out onto the great meadow in the park where parents join hands to form a tunnel or doors in a large circle, through which we pass singing. We conclude our little processions in the middle of the circle, and finish with an evening song before going home.

On the following days – as long as the weather is dry and the wind is not blowing – the gnome lights are still burning in the early morning when children arrive, and they go out as the day brightens. Very simple things can awaken wonder in children.

During free play in the mornings, from now on we light little lanterns made of cheese boxes or glass jars with tissue paper stuck on and – as far as possible – avoid switching the electric lights on. The children all carefully collect a lantern when they arrive and carry it to where they want to be busy. This gives a special atmosphere to play, and really allows the children to experience the semi-gloom.

# Thanksgiving [42]

Harvest festivals have been celebrated since ancient times throughout the world as a way of giving thanks (see 'Harvest Time', p. 109), and the Thanksgiving festival celebrated in the US on the fourth Thursday of November is one example. The popular (though disputed) version of the beginnings of the American Thanksgiving is the harvest celebration of the pilgrims and the Indigenous Americans in the autumn of 1621. North American colonists in the newly established village of Plymouth had suffered a difficult winter and they held a feast with the indigenous Wampanoag people who had made it possible for them to survive.

For most American households the Thanksgiving celebration has lost much of its original significance. We can remediate the consumer holiday it has become by creating a Thanksgiving gathering and feast in kindergarten for the children and their families, where we give a living example of gratitude and joy for what we have and what we can share together.

## Preparing in kindergarten

In kindergarten, planting in the spring, watering and weeding for many months, and then harvesting in the autumn is preparation for Thanksgiving. Throughout the growing year there are opportunities to bring reverence and gratitude to the earth and sun and wind and rain. And that is magnified at Thanksgiving time when the harvest is in.

Gathering in thanks and reverence for the harvest seems a perfect pedagogical activity for young children. In some kindergartens the children and teachers prepare a feast to share with parents. In kindergarten, every day is about reverence and gratitude and this day is an opportunity to join with the wider social setting in thankfulness. Additionally, a kindergarten can prepare cranberry sauce for children to take home for their families.

Another wonderful activity as preparation for a Thanksgiving gathering is cleaning. Guests are coming so we can do a more thorough clean than we do each day and week. A bonus of this activity is that it serves as a cleaning preparation for the Advent season as well. The tradition at schools in the US is to have a school holiday on Thanksgiving and the day after, and sometimes even for the entire week in which Thanksgiving falls. When the children return to kindergarten it is Advent time.

A practice in many kindergartens is celebrating the month of November as a time to experience and learn about Indigenous Americans, including stories, songs and crafts. It can appear as an attempt to teach history to some degree, and teach about cultures that may be different from the children's own. A more developmentally appropriate time for this opportunity might be eighth grade. I haven't chosen to do this in my kindergarten. I don't want to attempt to teach cultural literacy or history in early childhood, or set aside a particular time of year to offer such cultural enrichment. I would prefer to simply tell the story and let its cultural flavour say all that needs to be spoken to the children.

Slowly Advent approaches and we start the first activities of the 'big clean' as described in the section on 'Advent and Christmas' (p. 19). Thus closes the circle of the seasons, with which we can connect a little more strongly every year.

# Birthdays

## Creating the mood ourselves

Below we will discuss two events which we celebrate in a festive and fitting way quite independently of the season. They belong in the most individual way to our human biography, as the beginning and end of our earthly existence. These are the two thresholds which we cross: at birth, or conception, on the one hand – our 'earthly birth'; and at death on the other – our 'heavenly birthday'.

Old tales about the stork who brings a newborn child are usually dismissed with a smile today. And yet they contain deep wisdom, as we suggested in the section on Whitsun (see p. 84). The image of the stork was never to do with physical birth alone, but indicated that at a child's birth the soul and spirit descend from heavenly realms to earth. In relation to this process of the spirit connecting with the body, we speak of 'incarnation' – or in other words 'entry into flesh'. From this perspective, of the incarnation of the spirit, the unique nature of every human being becomes comprehensible. The body that we physically inherit from our parents takes up a spiritual being. This increasingly penetrates the body as children develop, coming to ever clearer expression in the child's individual character and biography.

Science, which gives us far-reaching and illuminating insights into human development from conception to death, is unable to tell us anything about our spiritual origins and nature. For this we would need a science that goes beyond matter to include the human spirit – a spiritual science such as anthroposophy, which Rudolf Steiner initiated at the beginning of the twentieth century. By this means we can renew our relationship with the inexhaustible truths contained in ancient myths and legends.

In a quite natural way we can help young children, who have recently left the heavenly realms and are awakening more each day within the sensory world, to preserve their connection with the spiritual world. We can tell them about their origins and journey to the earth, thus strengthening what already lives in them. When we clothe these stories in true images, they can echo children's pre-birth experiences, and give them a sense of security here on earth.

It all depends on us only telling children things that we feel are profound truths, which we can express with inner certainty. Sometimes children help us here through their unselfconscious and open way of asking questions; or they may surprise us with their spontaneous comments. Children often have a capacity to perceive the inner efforts and outlook of grown-ups they know well and trust.

## Celebrating birthdays in kindergarten

The birthday child arrives at kindergarten in joyful expectancy, bringing a little basket from home containing a small gift for each child. This may be two or three nuts, a couple of raisins and perhaps a fruit-jelly sweet or a home-baked biscuit. In many kindergartens children bring a birthday cake, or a cake may even be baked in the group. In discussion with parents we have decided to keep our usual morning snack, adding the contents of the little gifts as a starter or dessert. In summer or autumn, birthday children also sometimes bring a little basket containing fruits from the garden. The chief thing here is the gesture of being allowed to share something out. And there is likely to be cake anyway at home in the afternoon.

After the free-play period, while the last bit of clearing up is going on, we place the birthday table in the middle of the room with chairs around it and put a yellow cloth over the birthday chair. Once they've been to the washroom, all the children want to watch what's happening or help decorate the birthday table. Everything we need is in its usual place, easy for children and the teacher to reach. On the birthday tablecloth we first put a round disc of gold cardboard to protect against any drops of wax. On this we place the big 'life candle' and around it candles representing each year of the child's life, along with a vase of seasonal flowers or, in winter, a flowering pot plant. Place is found for the little bell, candle snuffer and the basket of gifts which the birthday child has brought; and finally also a small present wrapped in a silk cloth.

By now all the children have gathered, and the birthday child can be clothed in a golden-yellow birthday cloak and a golden crown (made from gold cardboard, about 3 cm, 1 in, wide, the top cut in a crown pattern). The birthday child can now go with two friends to wait outside the door. When the candles are burning and the bell rings, the children are greeted as they enter with a birthday song, such as the one given below, which we accompany with rocking gestures:

Waken sleeping butterfly,
Burst your narrow prison;
Spread your golden wings and fly
For the sun has risen.

Birthday sun break through the clouds,
Shine on joy and sorrow;
Life and light for earth today;
Star of love tomorrow.[43]

The song is followed by 'violin' or 'flute' music on imitated instruments, to which we sing, 'Good morning dear sunshine'.

Now the birthday story begins, which first tells of the child's journey to earth: how they left the golden house in heaven where God lives and, accompanied by their angel, was led past many stars to their family. It goes on to tell of the many joyful preparations in the parents' house, for example how the cradle or Moses basket was prepared, the special blanket and swaddling clothes, the warm, woollen jacket and hat. The story ends with the parents or carers looking into the baby's cradle and wondering what the loveliest name for their child would be; and then the child's name is spoken.

This story is the centrepiece and also highpoint of our little celebration. And although the images in the story are the same each time, the nuances can be subtly different. The story is essentially the same when children have been adopted and fostered or have different family structures. We can still trust that wise guidance has led them to the right family or carers.

If I notice that certain children are harbouring special questions about their birth, I try to take account of this by expanding the story a little. Most birthday children gaze at the teacher with big eyes as they tell the story, and one can sense how it deeply touches and satisfies them.

After the story, the birthday child may unwrap their present and walk around with it to show everyone, while we sing the corresponding song. After receiving a present, the birthday child may now give to others by placing a little gift in the hands of each child. Depending on circumstances we open the gift immediately or later at snack time. Finally, the birthday child puts out the year candles, leaving the life candle burning.

This birthday celebration takes place in the mornings when we would usually have our rhythmic or ring games. On such days we dispense with them so that the children are not overtaxed and don't lose any valuable free-play time.

To end the kindergarten morning, we often play the social game of 'fruit-sweet hide and seek'.

It is the custom in another kindergarten group for the kindergarten teacher to make each birthday child a small flower wreath from seasonal flowers. This is placed on a circle of gold cardboard, with the life candle in the middle and around it the year candles. Around these, in turn, the children place a decorative circle of small crystals. This initial work of the teacher in the morning often stimulates some of the children to make their own small wreaths and to celebrate dolls' birthdays in the doll corner.

When a child's birthday falls in the holidays, we naturally celebrate it when kindergarten begins again. And if there are several holiday birthdays, we celebrate them in order on subsequent days so that no children miss out on their birthday celebration. If two birthdays fall on the same day, we set up two birthday tables and tell the birthday story twice.

## Small birthday presents

Without any hard-and-fast rule, we choose a gift that seems suitable for the birthday child from the list below. We also try to ensure that the gift the following year can represent a small advance. Almost all these gifts are to be found in the book, *Toymaking with Children.* [44]

- Three to five gnomes on a round 'carpet' or in a large shell
- Small sheep sewn from a piece of leather
- Bark boats with one or two gnomes
- A pine-cone bird
- A standing doll (shepherd, or mother with child in a sling)
- A small knotted doll in a fabric or sheepskin bed (total length around 18 cm, 7 in).
- Treasure sacks, measuring around 11 x 9 cm (4 1/4 x 3 1/2 in) and containing, for instance, a small candleholder made of wood, or a shell with a tiny candle, several beautiful shells, beautiful stones or glass marbles, small pine cones and two gnomes. Six-year-olds especially love these sacks, and like using them to create a little gnome landscape.

## Birthdays at home

It can sometimes feel daunting to face the challenge of organising a child's birthday party at home.

First, it's good to think about who is to be invited. A younger kindergarten child of four or five, whose friends frequently change, may, if asked, wish to add new names to their list on a daily basis. If you don't yet know the other children and friends well, it's worth discussing this with the kindergarten teacher. It's helpful to invite only as many children as the number of years celebrated. The child will eagerly help make the invitation cards.

When children arrive, they could first gather round the birthday table, decorated only with birthday candles and flowers, and place their little presents on it. After a birthday song, the birthday child can take time to unwrap the presents slowly, while the others share in the surprise and pleasure. As this happens, a grown-up might take the wrapping paper and ribbons and fold them up carefully. It's good to avoid presents being ripped open too hurriedly and paper being thrown away carelessly. For this reason we always suggest avoiding sticky tape and difficult knots.

Depending on circumstances, you might go out for a walk, perhaps involving a treasure hunt. There are always magicians who bury their treasure and then can't remember where they hid it. When the magician goes through the bushes, sometimes a bit of his ragged cloak gets caught (red strips of crêpe-paper) and so we can see where he went and perhaps find the treasure. Depending on the season and the age of the children, the treasure might involve various materials which can later be used to make something: a box with modelling wax; a sack containing coloured wool; candles for decorating; coloured pieces of felt with sewing yarn for a pin cushion or pin book; transparency paper and little cheese boxes for lanterns; small boxes to paint and make into treasure chests, and so on.

Next perhaps it's time for the birthday tea with cake, juice or milkshake at a festive table. And then of course the children will love to play games together. After this, depending on circumstances, they might start making something with the 'treasure' material, with help if necessary from the grown-ups. Otherwise they can take these materials home with them.

Finally, there might be a small puppet show, or a parent could read a fairy tale (if possible beside an open fire); or otherwise there might simply be a quieter game. Depending on the season, the party might end with a lantern procession.

Of course things can also be organised in a quite different way, so that celebrations begin with the birthday tea, followed by games and other activities. Everyone will find what works best for their family.

The success of a children's birthday depends a good deal on planning and preparation. (There will always, also, be unexpected situations that require a spontaneous response.) A highly enjoyable and satisfying birthday can be organised with few and simple means.

Of course it requires special effort to arrange such a celebration, but this will be well rewarded by the children's enjoyment and happiness. Children will later look back thankfully on their lovely birthday party as a wellspring of creativity.


## 'Heavenly birthday'

Following our discussion of birthdays, let's also consider that other threshold which we cross at the end of life. The certainty with which we welcome children from pre-birth existence can also lead us to certainty about continued spiritual existence after death. Anthroposophy can give us clear insight into this life after death, through to the preparation of a new birth.[45] With this outlook – that we live on in spirit after death – we can find the right words to speak to children about the death of close family members, such as a grandparent or sibling. We don't need lots of words, but the ones we use should be vivid and pictorial. Young children are still very close to the world of spirit, and they receive such realities in the most natural way. We might talk about the angel who is now leading Grandpa back into heaven, or say that God called Grandpa away; and that now we can accompany the continuing journey of this beloved person with our love and memory.

On certain days we might place a flower and picture in a special place as well. If it arises, or if children ask, we could say a few words about the person's life or their journey through heaven. In this way, quite naturally, we can stay connected with someone who has died, and also nurture this connection with children. For instance, in a family with several children, one of whom had died, the question was sometimes asked, 'How many brothers and sisters do you have?' And the spontaneous reply was, 'Five sisters and a little brother in heaven.'[46]

On occasions when a parent or sibling of a kindergarten child has died, I have lit a candle at a suitable moment – for instance before telling a story – and spoken to the children very briefly about the 'heavenly birthday'.

The question repeatedly arises as to whether one should take pre-school children to a funeral. I advise against it. It seems to me more fitting to keep burial, which a child cannot yet really understand, as a mystery over which a veil is drawn. Children will form their own changing and living pictures – as they do when listening to fairy tales.

When familiar people are suddenly no longer around, and we tell children that they have gone back to heaven, this is a quite self-evident thing for them, and at the same time a vivid picture which they can grasp without confusion.

However, this advice is only very general, and our own sensitivity must guide us in questions relating to the most personal, intimate things. If children *are* taken to a funeral, the outlook and picture described above can still surround and support them. Justified deep mourning or grief at the loss of a loved person can then transform into inner certainty and trust in the divine world of spirit.

# Afterword

The journey through the year and its festivals allows us to experience how the earth passes through a great cyclical respiration as the seasons change. In spring begins the process of exhalation, which culminates at midsummer. Just as our soul and spirit leave our body in deep sleep, the earth organism is now asleep and given up to cosmic phenomena. Then this reverses and the earth soul slowly returns to itself until midwinter – just as we do when we awaken. This great breathing rhythm of the earth is apparent in the living processes at work in plants and animals.[47]

Due to the fact that Christ connected his being with the earth and humanity, the seasonal festivals have acquired new meaning. It's up to us to grasp this meaning ever more profoundly – or in other words, to seek the connections between the divine-spiritual and physical world, and to imbue our festivals with these insights. Anthroposophy can help us greatly in this endeavour, and slowly lead us towards greater inner certainty.

Over the years the festivals in our kindergarten have undergone various changes, whenever new insights suggested them. I hope that everyone will therefore feel encouraged to engage creatively, in their own way, with the Christian festivals through their own study of the spiritual realities at work in them, and thus develop new forms of celebration.

# Endnotes

1. Rudolf Steiner, *The Cycle of the Year as Breathing Process of the Earth*.
2. Karl König, *Calendar of the Soul: A Commentary*. König's commentary on Rudolf Steiner's work.
3. In Rudolf Steiner, *Breathing the Spirit*, translated by Matthew Barton.
4. Rudolf Steiner, translated by Matthew Barton.
5. Christian Morgenstern, translated by Matthew Barton.
6. For more on cleaning and tidying activities in kindergarten, see Freya Jaffke, *Work and Play in Early Childhood*.
7. Helene Jacquet, *Christmas Plays from Oberufer*.
8. In Steiner-Waldorf schools, the teachers traditionally act these plays each year as a gift to the children.
9. For further instructions on making Advent calendars, see Thomas Berger, *The Christmas Craft Book*.
10. **For making figures out of beeswax** we use 100% pure beeswax and add wool grease (suint) to it, which allows the wax to stay softer for longer, and is easier to shape in a child's hand.
    Preparation (sufficient quantity for 25 children):
    500 g (1 lb) beeswax and 30 g (1 oz) wool grease (from a chemist).
    Place the wax in an enamel bowl and allow to become fluid in an oven at 70°C (150°F) or in a bath of hot water. Then remove the bowl and stir in the wool grease with a stick. Leave for a while. As soon as the surface and the edges start to harden, scoop out teaspoons of the wax and loosely pile on a sheet of foil. When the bowl is empty, the loose mound of beeswax is put back into it. An hour to an hour and a half before we give the wax to the children for modelling, we put the bowl back in the oven at 50°C (120°F). Now the warm air can stream through the wax, and we can give each child a little warm, supple wax to hold and shape without them depleting their own warmth. If you don't have a stove in the kindergarten you can order golden-yellow modelling wax from the Stockmar company instead. This contains various substances that stop it being as hard as 100% pure beeswax and can also be lightly pre-warmed on a radiator or close to a heat source.
11. In Germany, presents are often said to come from 'the Christ Child'.
12. See also Freya Jaffke, *Work and Play in Early Childhood*.
13. Thomas Berger, *The Christmas Craft Book*.
14. Ibid.

15. **Recipe for quark-flour dough:**
    200 g (7 oz) fat (butter or margarine); 250 g (9 oz) low-fat quark; 250 g (9 oz flour) plus extra flour for dusting the work surface. Knead the ingredients together well. Form small items on a greased baking tray and bake for 20–25 minutes at 200°C (400°F), removing before they go brown.
16. From Heather Thomas, *A Journey Through Time in Verse and Rhyme.*
17. Translated from German kindergarten study materials by Matthew Barton.
18. Goethe, *Faust* Part 2, mountain ravines; the Chorus mysticus.
19. See, for instance, Rudolf Steiner lecture on April 3, 1920, published in *The Festivals and Their Meaning.*
20. See also Freya Jaffke, *Work and Play in Early Childhood.*
21. Translated by Matthew Barton.
22. Due to varying term dates between countries, the Easter celebration in kindergarten can be adapted to suit different timetables, and may be held before Easter.
23. **Easter egg recipes:**
    To make 10–12 eggs: 1 tablespoon mashed almonds or other nuts; 1 tablespoon honey; 3 tablespoons rusk flour or fine oatflakes; 1 tablespoon carob. Mix ingredients well and form the eggs with moist hands, then roll them in rusk flour and wrap in silver foil.
    To make approx. 175 eggs: 500 g (1 lb) dates; 500 g (1 lb) figs; 500 g (1 lb) pears; 500 g (1 lb) apricots; 500 g (1 lb) grated nuts; 4 lemons. Put the dry fruit to soak, then remove stones and feed through a mincer. Add the grated nuts and lemon juice, then add enough rusk flour until dry enough not to stick to hands. Form eggs and wrap in silver foil. Keep refrigerated.
24. In Rudolf Steiner, *Breathing the Spirit.*
25. Emil Bock, *The Rhythm of the Christian Year.*
26. See Rudolf Steiner, *The Cycle of the Year as Breathing Process of the Earth.*
27. Karl König, *Calendar of the Soul: A Commentary.* König's commentary on Rudolf Steiner's work.
28. In Rudolf Steiner, *Breathing the Spirit.*
29. This relates to a Grimm's fairy tale about a flower, which the legend says Mary used as a glass.
30. From Marianne Garff, *Es plaudert der Bach*, translated by Matthew Barton.
31. Ibid.
32. From Heather Thomas, *A Journey Through Time in Verse and Rhyme.*
33. This is known as 'The Legend of Knockgrafton', and is an Irish story.
34. The Grimm's stories *The Three Feathers* or *The Queen Bee* are well suited for this festival.

35. See Rudolf Steiner, *The Child's Changing Consciousness as the Basis of Pedagogical Practice*, Lecture 6.

36. **Making dried apple rings:**
Peel apples (preferably winter / late season apples) and remove the core with a corer. Dry unsprayed peels and cores for making tea. Slice the apples into approx. 5 mm ([1/4] in) slices and arrange loosely on a thin stick that fits exactly into the oven rails. The slices should not touch each other. Usually there will be room for 10–15 sticks in the oven at a time. Leave the oven door open a crack by inserting a spoon into the door, so that moisture can escape. Allow to dry for around 10–15 hours at 70°C (150°F). (In kindergarten we heated the oven throughout two mornings, but turned it off in between.) If necessary place the rings on a baking tray outside the oven to dry a little more, and then pack in sandwich bags and store for the winter. Naturally one can also thread the apple rings on strings and hang them up to dry instead.

37. Potato men are made from small and medium-sized potatoes. They are carefully brushed clean then sliced in half and placed cut-side down on a greased baking tray. Cook in the oven at 200°C (400°F) for about 30–40 minutes, then eat warm with the peel on.

38. In Alexander Carmichael, *Carmina Gadelica*.

39. The lower right arm is held vertically upright in front of the body. The elbow rests in the left palm.

40. The section on Halloween was written by Stephen Spitalny, a kindergarten teacher in the United States.

41. For a full description of how to make lanterns see Thomas Berger, *The Christmas Craft Book*.

42. The section on Thanksgiving was written by Stephen Spitalny, a kindergarten teacher in the United States.

43. From Brien Masters, *The Waldorf Songbook*.

44. Freya Jaffke, *Toymaking with Children*.

45. See Rudolf Steiner, *Life Between Death and Rebirth*; Rudolf Steiner, *Man's Being, His Destiny and World-Evolution*.

46. On this subject, see also William Wordsworth's poem, 'We Are Seven'.

47. See Rudolf Steiner, *The Cycle of the Year as Breathing Process of the Earth*.

# Bibliography and Further Reading

## General

Barz, Brigitte, *Festivals with Children*, Floris Books, Edinburgh.

Bock, Emil, *The Rhythm of the Christian Year*, Floris Books, Edinburgh.

Jacquet, Helene (ed.), *Christmas Plays from Oberufer*, Rudolf Steiner Press, Forest Row.

Jaffke, Freya, *Work and Play in Early Childhood*, Floris Books, Edinburgh.

Jenkinson, Sally, *The Genius of Play*, Hawthorn Press, Stroud.

König, Karl, *Calendar of the Soul: A Commentary*, Floris Books. Edinburgh.

Meyer, Rudolf, *The Wisdom of Fairy Tales*, Floris Books, Edinburgh.

Oldfield, Lynne, *Free to Learn*, Hawthorn Press, Stroud.

Steiner, Rudolf, *The Cycle of the Year as Breathing Process of the Earth* (GA 223), Rudolf Steiner Press, Forest Row.

—, *Breathing the Spirit*, Sophia Books (2007) & Rudolf Steiner Press (2002).

—, *The Child's Changing Consciousness as the Basis of Pedagogical Practice*, Lecture 6, Anthroposophic Press, Massachusetts.

—, *The Festivals and Their Meaning*, Rudolf Steiner Press, Forest Row.

—, *Life Between Death and Rebirth* (GA 140), Anthroposophic Press, Massachusetts.

—, *Man's Being, His Destiny and World-Evolution*, Anthroposophic Press, Massachusetts.

## Crafts and Activities

Berger, Thomas, *The Christmas Craft Book*, Floris Books, Edinburgh.

Berger, Thomas & Petra, *Crafts Through the Year: How to Make Traditional Gifts and Decorations for Every Season*, Floris Books, Edinburgh.

Egholm, Frank, *Easy Wood Carving for Children: Fun Whittling Projects for Adventurous Kids*, Floris Books, Edinburgh.

Guéret, Frédérique, *Crafting Magical Window Stars: How to Make Beautiful Paper Stars*, Floris Books, Edinburgh.

Jaffke, Freya, *Toymaking with Children*, Floris Books, Edinburgh.

van Leeuwen, M. & Moeskops, J., *The Nature Corner*, Floris Books, Edinburgh.

Petrash, Carol, *Earthwise: Environmental Crafts and Activities with Young Children*, Floris Books, Edinburgh.

Reinhard, Rotraud, *Crafting a Felt Farm: A Waldorf Project For All Ages*, Floris Books, Edinburgh.

Schafer, Christine, *Magic Wool Fairies: How to Make Seasonal Fairies and Angels*, Floris Books, Edinburgh.

—, *Magic Wool Mermaids and Fairies: How to Makes Seasonal Standing Figures*, Floris Books, Edinburgh.

## Stories, poetry and songs

Carmichael, Alexander, *Carmina Gadelica*, Floris Books, Edinburgh.

Drescher, Daniela, *An llustrated Treasury of Grimm's Fairy Tales*, Floris Books, Edinburgh.

Grimm, *A Favorite Collection of Grimm's Fairy Tales*, Floris Books, Edinburgh.

Kutsch, Irmgard & Walden Brigitte, *Spring and Summer Nature Activities for Waldorf Kindergartens*, Floris Books, Edinburgh.

—, *Autumn and Winter Nature Activities for Waldorf Kindergartens*, Floris Books, Edinburgh.

Lockie, Beatrys, *Bedtime Storytelling*, Floris Books, Edinburgh.

Marlys Swinger (ed.), *Sing through the Seasons*, Plough Publishing House, New York & Sussex.

Masters, Brien, *The Waldorf Song Book*, Floris Books, Edinburgh.

Matterson, Elizabeth (ed.), *This Little Puffin: Nursery Songs and Rhymes*, Puffin, London.

Mellon, Nancy, *Storytelling with Children*, Hawthorn Press, Stroud.

Thomas, Heather (ed.), *A Journey Through Time in Verse and Rhyme*, Floris Books, Edinburgh.

Floris Books

For news on all the latest books, and
exclusive discounts, join our mailing list at:

florisbooks.co.uk/signup

*And* get a FREE book
with every online order!

*We will never pass your details to anyone else.*